Longman Intermediate Listening Series
Book 1

KAREN HUNTER ANDERSON

KATHLEEN BRUEGGING

JOHN LANCE

CONTENTS

ISBN: 0 582 79790 X

Sponsoring Editor: Arley Gray
Project Editor: Lyn McLean
Cover and Design: Piedad Palencia
Illustrations: Marlies Merk Najaka

First printing 1983

Longman
95 Church Street
White Plains, New York 10601

6 7 8 9 10-AL-9594939291

INTRODUCTION

MISSING PERSON is a new and exciting approach to listening. The text is designed to:

Encourage the development of *listening strategies*.

Challenge students with *listening-centered problem-solving* activities.

Motivate students with a suspenseful mystery story that captures their interest and helps them improve listening skills at the same time.

MISSING PERSON consists of a book containing twelve lessons, a tapescript of all recorded material, an answer key and an accompanying cassette.

HOW TO TEACH MISSING PERSON

Here are some procedures for teaching **MISSING PERSON**. You may want to modify them to suit your own teaching style.

To begin each lesson have students look at the opening illustration, discuss what has already happened, and make predictions about what might happen next. Then, do the pre-listening exercises. (LISTENING WITH A PURPOSE, PREDICTING, or PRE-PARING TO LISTEN) These exercises help students understand the dialog by focusing their attention on important points they should listen for. Look at DO YOU KNOW THESE WORDS? the vocabulary gloss that explains the meaning of some important vocabulary that might be difficult for students. Then have students listen to the dialog recorded on the cassette and complete LISTENING FOR IMPORTANT DETAILS to see if they have understood the important points of the dialog. If the students aren't able to complete all the items, play the tape again or divide the dialog into sections and give students additional information to guide their listening.

LISTENING FOR LANGUAGE is a cloze dictation exercise. The words that have been deleted are items that are important for understanding the global meaning or function of what is being said. These exercises can be done as traditional dictations, or students can first predict what goes in the blank and then listen to the dialog to test their predictions.

In other exercises such as LISTENING FOR MAIN IDEAS, LISTENING AND MAK-ING INFERENCES, LISTENING FOR SEQUENCE OF EVENTS, and LISTENING FOR DIFFERENT POINTS OF VIEW, the goal of the practice is evident from the title. Directions for how to do the practice are provided under the title. LISTENING AND FUNCTION PRACTICE gives oral and written practice of important functions such as introducing, ordering in a restaurant, and making suggestions. Students fill in the blanks to complete the conversation and then practice it with a partner.

READING AND LISTENING FOR SPECIFIC INFORMATION is a multi-skill prob-lem-solving exercise. At the end of each episode the students read a diary entry that summarizes the main events and adds new information to the story. They then listen to a short dialog or monolog, synthesize the information from the reading and listening passage and use it to complete a task. WHAT DO YOU THINK? is the final exercise in each lesson. Students express their opinions about what has happened so far and speculate about what will happen next.

The Cassette contains the recorded material from each unit. This material is repeated in the tapescript at the back of the Student's Book. For some practices it is essential to play the tape, and these are marked with the symbol: For others it may be helpful to remind students of the content of the story by playing the tape.

AT THE AIRPORT

Kim, Terry, Mike and Tony are all students at Middletown College in Miami. They decide to visit Washington, D.C. together at the end of their summer vacation. They meet at the baggage claim at Washington National Airport on Friday, August 24.

LISTENING WITH A PURPOSE

Listen to the conversation and look for the answer to these questions.

1. Where did Tony go after he got off the plane?
2. What does Tony's suitcase look like?
3. What does Terry's suitcase look like?

Do You Know These Words?

baggage claim – where you pick up your suitcase after you get off the airplane

snack bar – an informal restaurant where you can get hamburgers, hot dogs, Cokes, etc.

LISTENING FOR IMPORTANT DETAILS

Circle *True* or *False*.

1. Mike likes to eat.   *True*   *False*

2. Terry's suitcase looks like Tony's.   *True*   *False*

3. Tony's friends think he is somewhere in the airport.   *True*   *False*

4. Someone steals Tony's suitcase.   *True*   *False*

5. There aren't many people at the airport.   *True*   *False*

6. Ray tries to catch the man who took Tony's suitcase.   *True*   *False*

LISTENING FOR LANGUAGE 📼

Listen to the conversation and fill in the blanks.

MIKE: Terry, _____ you and Tony fly in together?
1

TERRY: Yes, we _____ . But when we _____ off the
2   3

plane, Tony went to _____ some aspirin. That
4

_____ quite a while ago and he still hasn't come
5

back.

MIKE: Well, here _____ the baggage now.
6

TERRY: Let's _____ Tony's suitcase for him.
7

KIM: What _____ it look like?
8

TERRY: _____ a small green one, like _____ .
9   10

LISTENING FOR MAIN IDEAS

There are four people at the airport. Draw lines to connect the people who knew each other before.

LISTENING AND FUNCTION PRACTICE

Part 1. *Making introductions.* Last spring, Kim introduced Tony to her friend Terry. Here are some things they said. Put them in the right order to fill in the blanks.

How about you?   Nice to meet you too.
It's nice to meet you.   This is my friend Terry.
I'd like you to meet Tony.

KIM: Terry, _____
                              1
             Tony, _____
                              2

TONY: _____
                              3

TERRY: _____
                              4
             Where are you from?

TONY: Right here in Miami. _____
                                                    5

TERRY: I'm from Miami too.

Part 2. Make your own introductions. Fill in the blanks and practice the conversation with two partners.

A: _____ , I'd like you to meet _____ .

        _____ , this is _____ .

B: _____ .

C: _____ .

B: Where are you from?

C: _____ . How about you?

B: I'm from _____ .

3

READING AND LISTENING FOR SPECIFIC INFORMATION

Read the first part of Terry's journal about her trip to Washington. Then listen to the conversation between Mike and a policeman. Mike's version is different from Terry's in one important way.

Friday

Today was supposed to be the first day of a fantastic vacation, but it has turned out to be a disaster. This afternoon Tony disappeared at the airport! Tony and I flew in together, and when we were on the plane he said he had a bad headache. After we landed, he went to buy some aspirin. I waited and waited for him at the baggage claim, but he didn't come back. In a little while Ray, Kim and Mike showed up. We waited for our bags and tried to figure out what had happened to Tony. Finally, Tony's bag came and we were going to get it, but just then a man came up and grabbed it and ran away with it. Ray chased him, but he couldn't catch him. Mike went to the police and told them all about Tony and the bag, but they couldn't do anything. Tony never came back, so we finally went to the hotel. I hope Tony is all right. I'm really worried, but I don't know what we can do.

🎧

Listen to the conversation between Mike and a policeman and circle the correct answer.

1. The policeman thinks the bag probably belongs to
   a. the man who took it.
   b. Tony.

2. The policeman thinks that Tony
   a. is in trouble.
   b. is all right.

3. Mike thinks that Tony
   a. is in trouble.
   b. is all right.

4. Mike is _____ about the policeman's suggestion.
   a. happy
   b. unhappy

Compare Terry's version with Mike's version. What piece of information is different?

_____

_____

Who is right?

_____

WHAT DO YOU THINK?

Discuss these questions in small groups or as a class.

- Where is Tony?
- Who stole Tony's suitcase? Why?

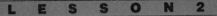

THE OREGON HOTEL

It's 5:00 P.M. and the students are still at the airport. Mike has just talked to the police about Tony and the stolen suitcase.

PREDICTING

What do you think will happen in this episode?

1. Mike, Ray, Kim and Terry will find Tony at the airport.
2. Tony's friends will find him at the hotel.
3. They will find Tony hurt.
4. Tony's friends won't find him anywhere.

Listen to the conversation and see if your prediction was correct.

Do You Know These Words?

identification tag – the suitcase tag with the name and address of the owner

initial – the first letter of a name. Tony Garcia's initials are T.G.

to page someone – to call someone's name over a loudspeaker.

LISTENING FOR IMPORTANT DETAILS

Circle *True* or *False.*

1. The police are going to look for the man who stole Tony's suitcase.   *True* *False*

2. Tony's friends take a taxi to the hotel.   *True* *False*

3. They know the man who takes them to the hotel.   *True* *False*

4. Tony's friends think he could still be at the airport.   *True* *False*

5. They are going to eat as soon as they put their suitcases in their rooms.   *True* *False*

LISTENING FOR LANGUAGE 📼

Listen to the conversation and fill in the blanks.

TERRY: Hey, what happened _____ that man who gave
                                             1

          _____ a ride?
              2

KIM: I _____ know. I guess _____ left.
                3   4

TERRY: We didn't even get _____ chance to thank him.
                                        5

RAY: That's too bad. _____ anyone get his name?
                                   6

MIKE: No, _____ never mentioned it. And he left
                  7

          _____ saying goodbye.
              8

RAY: You're right. How strange.

8

LISTENING FOR MAIN IDEAS

A stranger offers the students a ride to the hotel and mysteriously disappears before they can thank him. What do we know about him? Circle the things that apply to him.

   a. He's staying at the
       Oregon Hotel.
   b. He has a son.
   c. He is arriving from Miami.
   d. He drives a taxi.
   e. He has a car.
   f. He has friends at the hotel.
   g. He has a strange name.

LISTENING AND FUNCTION PRACTICE

Interrupting conversations and helping people. Complete the conversation with *a* or *b*.

Terry spent the summer in Miami with her family. When she was leaving for Washington, D.C. she asked for directions at the Miami Airport.

TERRY: Excuse me, I _____ overhearing your
                          1a. didn't like   b. couldn't help

        conversation. _____ Washing-
                          2a. Are you going to   b. Do you like

        ton, D.C.?

STRANGER: Yes, that's right.

TERRY: Could you tell me where Gate 21 is?

STRANGER: It's at the other end of the terminal. Why _____
                                         3a. do you

        _____ follow me? I'm _____
        b. don't you   4a. glad to meet you

        _____ .
        b. going that way

TERRY: Thank you, but my suitcase is too heavy to carry that
        far.

STRANGER: Let me _____ .

               5a. help you with it b. call a porter

TERRY: Oh no, I don't want to bother you. I'll just get a porter.

STRANGER: _____ ? Oh no, _____ .

     6a. Bother you b. A porter   7a. I insist b. I can't

TERRY: Well . . . OK. Thank you.

STRANGER: What's your name?

TERRY: Terry Blake.

STRANGER: I'm Jerry Anderson.

READING AND LISTENING FOR DIFFERENT POINTS OF VIEW

Read the second part of Terry's journal and listen to the conversation between Kim and Ray about someone they met at the airport.

Not everything that happened today was bad, though. One good thing was that we found out there are still some nice people in the world. While we were waiting at the airport trying to decide what to do, a man gave us a ride to our hotel. He said he had a son about our age and just wanted to help. I can't get over how nice he was. The police weren't very helpful, but this man, who didn't even know us, wanted to do something for us. It makes me feel good to know that even in a big city like Washington there are people who care for others.

Terry and Kim have a different opinion about this person. What's the difference? Circle the correct answer.

1. Terry is/isn't suspicious of the man who gave them a ride.
2. Kim is/isn't suspicious of the man who gave them a ride.
3. Ray agrees with Kim/Terry.

WHAT DO YOU THINK?

Discuss this question in small groups or as a class.

- Why do you think the man was so friendly at first and then left without saying goodbye?

DINNER TIME

By 6:00 P.M. the students have checked into the hotel. They decide to get something to eat while they're waiting to hear from Tony.

PREDICTING

Tony's friends are going to the hotel restaurant. Who will probably order the biggest dinner?

1. Kim   3. Ray
2. Mike   4. Terry

Why do you think so?
Listen to the conversation and see if your prediction was correct.

Do You Know These Words?

trash – things people throw away after using them, e.g., empty bottles, old newspapers
hotel confirmation slip – the piece of paper a hotel mails to a guest saying that a room has been reserved

LISTENING FOR IMPORTANT DETAILS

Circle the correct answer.

1. Where did the police find Terry's suitcase?
   - a. in a trash can at the airport   c. on the plane
   - b. in the Lost Baggage Office

2. Who doesn't order any food?
   - a. Mike   b. Kim   c. Terry

3. Where does Kim think they should look for Tony?
   - a. at the other hotels   b. at the hospital   c. at Acme

4. Why did the police call Terry?
   - a. They found her suitcase at the airport.
   - b. They found her purse.
   - c. They found Tony's suitcase.

5. Where are the students going?
   - a. to Terry's room   c. to another restaurant
   - b. to the airport

LISTENING FOR LANGUAGE 📼

Listen to the conversation and fill in the blanks.

MIKE: I'm worried _____ Tony. Maybe _____
                1   2
       really got sick.

KIM: Yeah, maybe _____ should check _____
                    3   4
       hospitals. Terry said he _____ bad on the plane.
                               5
       He _____ a sore throat and was really tired.
             6

MIKE: I _____ see why. He works twenty hours
         7
       _____ week at Acme and you _____ how
        8   9
       much he studies. I don't know how he _____ it.
                                       10

RAY: Here comes Terry.

KIM: _____ was on the phone?
      11

TERRY: The police! They _____ my suitcase in a trash can
                        12
       at the airport!

INTENSIVE LISTENING 📼

Listen to what the students order at the restaurant. Check
(√) what each person orders.

	MIKE	RAY	KIM
fried chicken dinner	____	____	____
an egg salad sandwich	____	____	____
two cheeseburgers	√	____	____
mashed potatoes and gravy	____	____	____
french fries	____	____	____
cheesecake	____	____	____
onion rings	____	____	____
a chocolate milkshake	____	____	____
diet cola	____	____	____
black coffee	____	____	____

LISTENING AND FUNCTION PRACTICE

Ordering. Complete Mike's order at the Airport Coffee Shop
with *a* or *b*.

WAITRESS: Are you ready to order?

MIKE: Yes, _____ two hot dogs _____ .
                 1a. I like b. I'd like   2a. please b. right now

WAITRESS: What do you want on them?

MIKE: Just _____ .
             3a. ketchup b. ketchup, mustard, tomato, onions and pickles

WAITRESS: What _____ to drink?
             4a. do you like b. do you want

MIKE: Coffee.

WAITRESS: With cream and sugar?

MIKE: _____ .
       5a. No, thank you b. No, I don't

WAITRESS: Would you like dessert?

MIKE: Yes, _____ some ice cream.
            6a. I like b. I want

WAITRESS: What flavor?

MIKE: Vanilla.

WAITRESS: _____
       7a. Is that all? b. Are you all right?

MIKE: Yes, thank you.

READING AND LISTENING FOR DIFFERENT POINTS OF VIEW

Here's a conversation between Terry and a policeman, and more of Terry's journal. Listen to the conversation and answer this question.

Why do you think Detective Sanderson is suspicious of Terry?

Terry and Detective Sanderson seem to have a different opinion about the suitcase. As you read, look for answers to these questions.

1. Why does Detective Sanderson ask so many questions?
2. Does Terry think she did anything wrong?

Things are getting stranger and stranger. By the time we got to the hotel, it was dinner time and we were all really hungry, so we went to the restaurant to get something to eat. We were just getting ready to order when I was called to the telephone. What a surprise! It was a detective from the Washington Police Department. First he asked me a lot of questions and then he said my suitcase had been found in a trash can at the airport. He wanted to know what was in it. I didn't have any idea what he was talking about. I told him my suitcase was up in my room. He said he had my suitcase and that he knew it was mine because the hotel confirmation slip was in it. I asked him whose suitcase I had, but he didn't know. Detective Sanderson seemed to think I had done something wrong, but I don't understand why he thinks that. All I did was pick up my own suitcase.

WHAT DO YOU THINK?

Discuss these questions in small groups or as a whole class.

- What do you know about Tony? What do you imagine?
- If Terry's suitcase is at the airport, whose suitcase is in her room?

AN INTRUDER

Terry receives a phone call from the police. The students rush up to her room to see whose suitcase is there.

LISTENING WITH A PURPOSE 📼

Listen to the conversation and look for the answer to these questions.

1. Who is in Terry's room?
2. What is in the suitcase?

Do You Know These Words?

to knock down – to make someone fall down

microfilm – film for photographing a page or letter in a very small size. The page can be read when it is made larger by a machine.

blueprints – photographic reproductions of architectural or industrial plans

LISTENING FOR IMPORTANT DETAILS

Circle *True* or *False*.

1. Terry and Kim's room is on the fifth floor.   *True*   *False*

2. Kim locked the door to her room.   *True*   *False*

3. Terry has Tony's suitcase in her room.   *True*   *False*

4. The man hits Terry on the head.   *True*   *False*

5. The man takes Terry's suitcase.   *True*   *False*

6. Terry and Tony have the same initials.   *True*   *False*

7. The students are going to tell the police about the microfilm in Tony's suitcase.   *True*   *False*

LISTENING FOR SEQUENCE OF EVENTS

Listen to the conversation and put the following events in the correct order.

_____ Mike opens Tony's suitcase.

__1__ A man breaks into Terry and Kim's room.

_____ The students get off the elevator.

_____ The students find a big envelope in

Tony's suitcase.

_____ A man knocks Terry down.

_____ Mike and Ray run after the man.

_____ Ray finds the door of Kim and Terry's room open.

_____ The students call the police.

_____ Mike finds Tony's red jacket in the suitcase.

LISTENING FOR LANGUAGE 📼

Listen to the conversation and fill in the blanks.

TERRY: _____ a man in here! Hey, _____ are you?
         1   2

        _____ are you doing with that suitcase?
         3

MIKE: Hey you! _____ back here! Come _____ ,
                   4   5

        Ray, let's see if we _____ catch him.
                         6

KIM: Terry, _____ you all right?
               7

TERRY: Oh, my head!

KIM: Here, let me _____ you up.
                 8

LISTENING AND FUNCTION PRACTICE

Offering to help. Mike and Terry were walking down the stairs and Terry slipped and fell. Use this list to complete their conversation.

Hey you!	Here we are.
That's right.	I'm OK now.
Did you hurt yourself?	Did you fall?
Let me help you up.	Oh, my foot.

MIKE: Terry! _____ You really fell hard.

TERRY: _____ I don't think I can stand up.

MIKE: _____ Here, give me your arm.

TERRY: Thanks. _____ I just felt a little dizzy.

MIKE: Maybe you need something to eat.

READING AND LISTENING FOR SPECIFIC INFORMATION

Read Terry's journal and listen to the conversation. Look for the answer to this question: *Who broke into Terry's room?*

After the phone call, I went back to get the others at the restaurant. I told them what Detective Sanderson had told me and they were all very excited. We rushed out of the restaurant and up to the room. When we got there, the door was open, which was strange because Kim had locked it when we left. We ran into the room and found a man there. He was going through my suitcase. When I tried to stop him, he knocked me down. I hit my head against a chair when I fell. As a matter of fact, it still hurts. Ray and Mike chased him to the elevator, but he got away. The strangest part was what came next. We looked in the suitcase and found out it was Tony's. Tony has the same initials as I do, so that was why I thought it was my suitcase. When we looked inside, we found an envelope with microfilm in it. We held the microfilm up to the light and saw what looked like blueprints on it. We're going to take it to the library tomorrow and find out what's really on it. I think it's a plan for a new kind of rocket. Also, we figured out that the man who was in the room looked a lot like the man who gave us the ride over to the hotel. I wonder who he is.

Listen to the conversation between Wilbur and Joe and answer the questions.

1. What is Joe's relationship to Wilbur? _____

2. Wilbur says he isn't a criminal. What does that mean about Joe and the others? _____

3. Is Wilbur a violent person? _____

WHAT DO YOU THINK?

Discuss this question in small groups or as a class.

- Why is the microfilm in Tony's suitcase?

THE PLANS

At 9:00 the next morning, the students take the microfilm to a nearby library. They want to use one of the microfilm machines to find out what is on the film.

PREPARING TO LISTEN

What do you know about microfilm?

1. Have you ever used a microfilm machine?
2. What does a microfilm machine look like?
3. How does it work?

Listen to the conversation to find out what is on the microfilm.

Do You Know These Words?

I can't make heads or tails of it. – I can't understand it.

chemical formulas – a combination of letters and numbers that shows what a substance is made of, e.g., H_2O, CO_2

battery – something used to create an electric current by a chemical reaction

LISTENING FOR IMPORTANT DETAILS

Circle _True_ or _False_.

1. The police think something awful has happened to Tony.   _True_   _False_

2. Mike often uses microfilm reading machines.   _True_   _False_

3. Kim knows how to work the microfilm reader.   _True_   _False_

4. Terry doesn't understand the microfilm.   _True_   _False_

5. The students are going back to the hotel after they visit the library.   _True_   _False_

6. Tony is an engineer at Acme Corporation.   _True_   _False_

7. The students are going to call Acme Corporation.   _True_   _False_

LISTENING FOR LANGUAGE 📼

Listen to the conversation and fill in the blanks.

KIM: Mike, you _did_ bring the microfilm, didn't you?

MIKE: Of course! I have _____ right here. How does this
1
stupid machine work? I can't get the microfilm to go in.

KIM: Here, let me show you. _____'s easy. You do
2
_____ like this.
3

MIKE: Will you look at _____ ! Why in the world did
4
Tony have something like _____ in his suitcase?
5

TERRY: Let me look. Good grief! What is that stuff? I can't make
heads or tails of _____ .
6

KIM: _____ are diagrams and chemical formulas for
7
some kind of battery.

LISTENING FOR MAIN IDEAS

Listen to the conversation. Check (√) the statements that describe the plans.

_____ The plans belong to Acme Electronics Corporation.

_____ The battery is inexpensive to produce.

_____ The battery weighs eight pounds.

_____ The battery charge lasts for 500 miles if the car is going at 55 miles per hour.

_____ The plans were made by Tony Garcia.

_____ The battery is six inches high.

_____ The battery is for a gasoline-powered car.

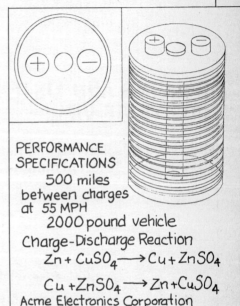

PERFORMANCE
SPECIFICATIONS
500 miles
between charges
at 55 MPH
2000 pound vehicle
Charge-Discharge Reaction
$$Zn + CuSO_4 \longrightarrow Cu + ZnSO_4$$
$$Cu + ZnSO_4 \longrightarrow Zn + CuSO_4$$
Acme Electronics Corporation

LISTENING AND FUNCTION PRACTICE

Asking for confirmation and asking for information. When Mike says "Boy, the police haven't been very helpful, have they?" he isn't asking for new information. He wants Terry to agree with him and confirm what he has said. But when Kim says, "You *did* bring the microfilm, didn't you?" she thinks the answer is yes, but she still wants Mike to give her an answer so that she knows for sure. Decide if the speaker is asking for confirmation or for information and circle the correct answer.

1. MIKE: Boy, the waitress sure has been slow, hasn't she?
   a. information   b. confirmation

2. TERRY: You left the key at the desk, didn't you?
   a. information   b. confirmation

3. MIKE: Terry, you *did* thank the librarian, didn't you?
   a. information b. confirmation

4. RAY: The people at the hotel are really nice, aren't they?
   a. information b. confirmation

5. TERRY: People wouldn't have to depend on the oil companies, would they?
   a. information b. confirmation

READING AND LISTENING FOR DIFFERENT POINTS OF VIEW

Read Terry's journal and listen to the conversation. Terry and Mike have a different opinion about Tony. What is the difference?

Saturday

After all the excitement yesterday evening, things finally calmed down. I guess we all thought someone might break into our rooms while we were sleeping. Nothing happened, though, and this morning we took the microfilm to a library to see what was on it. We were really surprised. It wasn't rockets at all. The film had blueprints on it for a new kind of battery. It's a battery for electric cars — cars that don't need gasoline. No wonder someone is trying to get hold of the plans. The film is from Acme Electronics, the firm Tony works for. What we don't understand is why Tony is mixed up in this. I hope he didn't steal the plans. Mike and Kim think that Tony was probably kidnapped by the people who are trying to get the plans and that he doesn't know anything about the microfilm. I hope they're right, but I'm not a 100 percent sure. It was a little mysterious the way he left to get that aspirin so fast. But Tony's such a great guy. He can't be a criminal.

Listen to the conversation between Kim and Mike. What did you find out from the journal and the conversation? Circle the correct answer.

1. Terry thinks that Tony   a. *is*   a criminal.
                    b. *might be*
                    c. *isn't*

2. Mike thinks that Tony   a. *is*   a criminal.
                    b. *might be*
                    c. *isn't*

3. Kim agrees more with   a. *Terry.*
                    b. *Mike.*

WHAT DO YOU THINK?

Discuss this question in small groups or as a class.

- Do you think Tony has been kidnapped?

ACME

The students have discovered that the microfilm contains plans from Acme Corporation, the company that Tony works for. They call Miami and speak to Dr. Franklin, head of the Acme research department.

PREDICTING

What do you think will happen in this episode?

1. What are Kim and Dr. Franklin probably talking about?
2. What do you think Dr. Franklin will tell Kim to do?

Listen to the conversation and see if your prediction was correct.

Do You Know These Words?

security man – a person employed to protect a business

scar – a mark left on the skin after an injury

LISTENING FOR IMPORTANT DETAILS

Circle the correct answers.

1. Dr. Franklin doesn't understand
    a. the plans for a battery.
    b. why Tony stole the plans.
    c. why Kim has the plans.
    d. all of the above

2. Dr. Franklin tells Kim
    a. Acme has plans for a battery.
    b. the battery plans are a secret.
    c. she's sending a security man.
    d. all of the above

3. What will the students do in the afternoon?
    a. Go look for Tony.
    b. Wait at the hotel for the security man.
    c. Go to the Smithsonian Institution.
    d. all of the above

4. The security man from Acme
    a. has information about Tony.
    b. probably stole the plans.
    c. will be at the hotel in the afternoon.
    d. none of the above

5. The man who is following the students
    a. has a scar on his face.
    b. was at the hotel earlier.
    c. was at the library.
    d. all of the above

LISTENING FOR LANGUAGE 📼

Listen to the conversation and fill in the blanks.

KIM: Yes, I think the plans are for some _____
                                          1
of battery.

DR. FRANKLIN: I don't understand what you're doing with

              _____ .
                  2

KIM: Our friend Tony Garcia works _____ your
                                        3

  company. He disappeared at the airport yesterday

  and we have _____ idea where he is. We
                          4

  found the _____ in his suitcase last night.
                     5

DR. FRANKLIN: In _____ suitcase! Where are the plans
                 6

  _____ ?
      7

KIM: I have them _____ me.
                  8

DR. FRANKLIN: Where are you _____ ?
                       9

KIM: At the Oregon Hotel, on K Street.

INTENSIVE LISTENING

Below is a list of famous places in Washington. Listen to the conversation and check (√) the places the students see on their walk.

____ The Washington Monument   ____ The White House

____ The National Gallery of Art   ____ The Reflecting Pond

____ The Lincoln Memorial   ____ The Smithsonian Institution

____ The Museum of Natural   ____ The Museum of Science
       History   and Technology

LISTENING AND FUNCTION PRACTICE

Making suggestions. **Look at Mike and Kim's conversation.**

RAY: What can we do until then?
MIKE: Let's get something to eat. I'm starved.
KIM: That's a good idea, but we really should go back to the hotel. We can eat there.
TERRY: OK. Let's go.

Complete these conversations with a suggestion and a response. Practice with a partner.

A: Let's _____ . I'm hungry.

B: That's a good idea, but _____ .

We can _____ .

C: OK.

A: I'm bored. Let's _____ .

B: That's a good idea, but _____ .

We can _____ .

C: OK.

READING AND LISTENING FOR SPECIFIC INFORMATION

Read Terry's journal and listen to the conversation.

As soon as we found out that the microfilm was from Acme Corporation, we called up the company. Kim spoke to a woman named Dr. Franklin. She said she would send a security man to pick it up later in the afternoon.

After we left the library, we decided to see a

few sights on the way back to the hotel. When we were going by the Smithsonian Institution, Kim noticed that a man with a scar on his face was following us. She said she recognized him because she'd seen him at the hotel and at the library. Then I realized that he was the man who ran off with my suitcase at the airport. We jumped into a taxi and I think we lost him. This vacation is getting scary. One thing I am sure of now, though, is that Tony couldn't be mixed up with these people.

Listen to the conversation between Dr. Franklin and the security man who is going to pick up the microfilm. What did you learn from the journal and the conversation? Circle *True* or *False*.

1. Terry thinks Tony stole the plans.   *True*   *False*

2. Tony has a poor work record at Acme Corporation.   *True*   *False*

3. Dr. Franklin thinks Tony is probably a member of the gang.   *True*   *False*

4. Dr. Franklin trusts all of the scientists who work at Acme Corporation.   *True*   *False*

5. Dr. Franklin thinks that it doesn't matter that she told Kim about the top secret plans.   *True*   *False*

WHAT DO YOU THINK?

Discuss this question in small groups or as a class.

- Do you think Tony stole the microfilm?

THE PICKUP

After returning from the library, the students ate lunch at the hotel and then Terry and Ray went to the police station to pick up her suitcase. By 6:00 P.M., they were all back at the hotel and Mike was hungry again.

LISTENING WITH A PURPOSE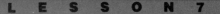

Listen to the conversation and look for the answers to these questions.

1. Who picks up the microfilm?
2. Why is Dr. Franklin's call such a surprise?

Do You Know These Words?

to think straight – to think clearly, without confusion

pepperoni – an Italian sausage, often put on pizza

to get in touch with – to contact someone

LISTENING FOR IMPORTANT DETAILS

Circle *True* or *False*.

1. Kim doesn't want to order a pizza.   *True*   *False*

2. Mike looks in the phone book for a place to order the pizza.   *True*   *False*

3. The students order three pizzas.   *True*   *False*

4. Terry doesn't feel well.   *True*   *False*

5. The man who took the microfilm is from the Acme Electronics Corporation.   *True*   *False*

6. The Acme security man calls Kim.   *True*   *False*

LISTENING FOR LANGUAGE 🔲

Listen to the conversation and fill in the blanks.

MIKE: Look, since we _____ to wait here for the security
                              1

man, why _____ we order a pizza? I'm so
                    2

_____ I can't think straight.
      3

KIM: That's _____ a bad idea. Here's the _____
               4   5

book.

MIKE: OK. Let's see now. Hmm. Here's a place that

_____ . Should we get a _____ or a large?
      6   7

RAY: The way you eat, I think we should get an _____
                                          8

large.

MIKE: OK.

LISTENING FOR SEQUENCE OF EVENTS 🔲

Listen to the conversation and put the following events in the correct order.

_____ Mike orders a pizza.

_____ A man takes the microfilm from the students.

_____ The students return to the hotel.

_____ Dr. Franklin calls.

_____ Terry complains about her headache.

_____ Mike and Ray run after the man who took the microfilm.

LISTENING AND FUNCTION PRACTICE

Part 1. _Distinguishing suggestions from other functions._ **Which of these sentences are suggestions about what to do? Mark the suggestions with an _S_.**

_____ Why don't we order a pizza?

_____ That's not a bad idea.

_____ I'd like to order an extra large pizza, please.

_____ The way you eat, I think we should get an extra large.

_____ I need your name, address and phone number.

Part 2. Fill in the blanks to make suggestions.

TERRY: Oh no! What are we going to do now?

KIM: _____ call the police right away.
          1a. Can I   b. We'd better

TERRY: _____ wait a little while to do that?
          2a. Why don't we   b. Let's

KIM: Why? I think _____ do it right away if they're
          3a. we should   b. let's

going to help Tony.

TERRY: I guess you're right. I just don't want to talk to that Detective

Sanderson again. He doesn't like me.

KIM: _____ saying we want to talk to the
　　　　4a. Why don't we   b. How about
Chief of Police? Sanderson isn't the chief.

TERRY: All right. But what if he doesn't believe us?

KIM: _____ just say we talked to Dr. Franklin at
　　　　5a. Let's   b. How about
Acme Electronics.

READING AND LISTENING FOR SPECIFIC INFORMATION

Read the next part of Terry's journal and listen to the conversation between Joe and Harry. Terry is mistaken about one fact. What is it?
Answer the questions.

1. At the end of this part of her journal, does Terry think that giving the microfilm to the wrong person was stupid?
2. What do you think?

I can't believe how stupid we were. We gave the film to the wrong person. We knew we lost the scar-faced man when we jumped into the taxi because we couldn't see him following us anymore. It wasn't hard to lose him. Ray waited outside the hotel to see if he would find us, but he didn't come.

We were expecting the security man around 6:00. He arrived and we gave him the film. We were really glad to get rid of it. But right after he left, Dr. Franklin called and said that the security man who had come to the door wasn't the real security man.

We all felt terrible. Actually, I guess we weren't so stupid at that. After all, Dr. Franklin did say the security man would be coming around 6:00. How were we to know that the man who came to the door wasn't the right person? We just wanted to get rid of the film.

Earlier that afternoon, Joe, the scar-faced man, called Harry, one of the gang members. Listen to their conversation and fill in the blanks.

1. Who is the boss of the gang? _____

2. Who is more violent, Joe or Harry? _____

3. How does Harry know that the security man is supposed to come late in the afternoon? _____

4. What was Terry wrong about? _____

WHAT DO YOU THINK?

Discuss these questions in small groups or as a class.

- Who was the man at the door? Why did he take the microfilm?
- Should Mike and Ray follow the man with the microfilm?

A WILD CHASE

Ray and Mike rush out of the hotel and see the man who took the microfilm going by in a black Chevy. They get a cab and follow him to the other side of town.

PREDICTING

What do you think will happen in this episode?

1. What will happen to Ray and Mike?
2. Will they catch the man who took the microfilm?

Listen to the conversation and see if your prediction was correct.

Do You Know These Words?

gate – a door in a wall used for entrance or exit

basement – the part of a house that is underground

to tie up – to tie someone's hands and feet with rope

LISTENING FOR IMPORTANT DETAILS

Circle *True* or *False*.

1. The man takes a cab to an old house.   *True*   *False*

2. The old house is near the hotel.   *True*   *False*

3. Mike gives the cab driver exactly $11.50.   *True*   *False*

4. The dog is in the house.   *True*   *False*

5. Mike and Ray think they see Tony inside of
   the house.   *True*   *False*

6. Mike eats his sandwiches.   *True*   *False*

LISTENING FOR LANGUAGE 📼

Listen to the conversation and fill in the blanks.

MIKE: Ray, where are we?

RAY: Don't worry. While you were _____ the cab driver
1
follow the car, I was _____ where we were going.
2

MIKE: We're quite a way from the hotel, _____ we?
3

RAY: We sure are. The guy _____ the car over there. Did
4
you see where he went _____ he got out?
5

MIKE: Yeah, he _____ into that old house.
6

RAY: The _____ with the brick wall around
7
_____?
8

MIKE: Yeah.

RAY: OK. _____ go.
9

LISTENING FOR DETAILS 📼

Listen to Ray and Mike's
description of the dog.
Which drawing best matches
their description?

A.

B.

C.

Now check (√) the char-
acteristics.

_____ has big ears
_____ has no teeth
_____ has no tail
_____ has no ears
_____ is all black
_____ has big teeth
_____ has a long tail
_____ is all white
_____ has strange spots

LISTENING AND FUNCTION PRACTICE

Expressing uncertainty. In this episode, Mike and Ray aren't sure
of what they see and hear. Mike says *"It sounds like a dog barking,"*
which means "I think it's a dog barking, but I'm not sure." Other
verbs can be used in the same way to show uncertainty. Some examples are

seem like   *smell like*   *sound like*
taste like   *look like*   *feel like*

Use these examples in the blanks below to show other things
that Ray and Mike could say.

1. That _____ a phone booth down the street.

   Let's call from there.

2. I don't know what's in this sandwich, but it's really good. It

   _____ cream cheese.

45

3. Be quiet! Do you hear that? It _____ some-one's coming.

4. I don't know about going in there, Ray. It _____ the right thing to do, but I'm still scared.

5. I can't see what's on top of this wall, but it _____ pieces of broken glass.

6. Someone was just here by the gate. It _____ whoever it was was smoking a cigarette.

READING AND LISTENING FOR DIFFERENT POINTS OF VIEW

Read Terry's journal and listen to the conversation between Mike and Ray. Terry and Mike have different opinions of their relationship. What is the difference?

After I called the police, Kim and I sat around killing time and talking about Tony, Mike and Ray. Kim asked me if I had ever gone out with Mike. I said no, but then I remembered that I did invite him to a Halloween party once and that we used to do a lot of things together with other friends of mine. Mike's like a brother to me. I've always been able to count on him if I have a problem. He used to tutor me in biology and math and I used to help him with his English papers. Then Kim asked me about Ray. I said I liked him and was glad she had invited him to come with us. Actually, I really like him a lot. When Kim introduced us at the airport, I thought he was really nice-looking. Since I knew we'd be spending the next few days together, I figured I could get to know him pretty well. It made the trip seem even more exciting. I think he likes me too. When that man knocked me down, he helped me up and asked me if I was OK. He seemed really concerned. Maybe he's like that with everybody. Well, we'll see . . . .

Answer the questions.

1. How does Terry feel about Mike? _____

2. How does Terry feel about Ray? _____

Mike and Ray are in a taxi following the man who has the microfilm. Listen to their conversation and circle *True* or *False*.

1. Terry doesn't have a serious boyfriend right now.   *True   False*

2. According to Mike, he and Terry were always just friends.   *True   False*

Terry and Mike have different opinions of the relationship they had. What is the difference? _____

_____

WHAT DO YOU THINK?

Discuss these questions in small groups or as a whole class.

- Are Mike and Ray in danger?
- Are Kim and Terry in danger?

BACK AT THE HOTEL

It's 7:00 P.M. and Terry and Kim are waiting for the real security man from Acme.

PREDICTING

Two people come to the hotel in this episode. Who do you think they will be?

1. _____

2. _____

Listen to the conversation and see if your prediction was correct.

Do You Know These Words?

Oh my gosh! – something you say when you're surprised

Darn! – something you say when you're angry

sneak – to move quietly so that no one can hear you

supposedly – not for sure

49

LISTENING FOR IMPORTANT DETAILS

Circle *True* or *False*.

1. The security man thinks Terry and Kim are trying to help Tony.   *True*   *False*

2. The security man has a gun.   *True*   *False*

3. The security man is tall and blond.   *True*   *False*

4. Terry gave the pizza man exactly $8.75.   *True*   *False*

5. Kim thinks Ray and Mike should go inside the house.   *True*   *False*

LISTENING FOR LANGUAGE 📼

Listen to the conversation and fill in the blanks.

SECURITY MAN: Hello. I'm ＿＿＿＿＿ Acme Electronics.
1

KIM: Oh, am I glad to ＿＿＿＿＿ you!
2

SECURITY MAN: I came to pick ＿＿＿＿＿ the microfilm.
3

TERRY: Well, we ＿＿＿＿＿ actually have it.
4

SECURITY MAN: What do you ＿＿＿＿＿ you don't have it?
5

KIM: What she means ＿＿＿＿＿ we accidentally
6
＿＿＿＿＿ it to the wrong person. A man came
7
to our door a little while ＿＿＿＿＿ . We
8
thought he was from Acme, so we gave
＿＿＿＿＿ the microfilm.
9

SECURITY MAN: What did he ＿＿＿＿＿ like?
10

KIM: He was tall ＿＿＿＿＿ blond.
11

LISTENING AND MAKING INFERENCES

Listen to Kim and Ray's telephone conversation. Fill in Ray's part of the conversation.

KIM: I'll get it. Hello?

RAY: _____

KIM: Ray! Where are you?

RAY: _____

_____

KIM: Did you find out anything?

RAY: _____

KIM: Where is he?

RAY: _____

KIM: Just a minute. Let me get a pencil. OK. I'm ready.

RAY: _____

KIM: Got it.

RAY: _____

_____

KIM: Ray, I don't think that's a good idea. Why don't you call—
Darn! He hung up.

LISTENING AND FUNCTION PRACTICE

Emphasizing. The question form is sometimes used for emphasis even though there is no question. When Terry says *"How could we be so stupid!"* she means *"We were very stupid."* *"Am I glad to see you!"* means *"I am very glad to see you."* Notice that an exclamation point (!) is used rather than a question mark (?).

Fill in the blanks with a real question or an emphatic form.

MIKE: I don't think we should go inside, Ray.

RAY: Why? _____
          1a. Are you frightened? b. Are you frightened!

MIKE: Yes, a little.

RAY: So am I. But we can't worry about ourselves.

_____
    2a. Am I worried about Tony? b. Am I worried about Tony!

MIKE: I am too. I sure would feel better if I had something to eat.

_____
    3a. Am I hungry? b. Am I hungry!

RAY: You're always hungry, Mike.

MIKE: Yeah, I guess you're right. I wish we were back at the hotel.

READING AND LISTENING FOR SPECIFIC INFORMATION 🔲

Listen to the conversation between the security man and a cab driver who picks him up at the airport. Then read the next part of Terry's journal. Terry is wrong about why the security man is late. What does Terry think and what is the real reason the security man doesn't get there in time to pick up the microfilm?

Listen and answer the questions.

1. Jim Whiteside is *a. nervous.   b. calm.*
2. Jim Whiteside is from *a. Washington.   b. Miami.*
3. The taxi driver knows *a. something   b. nothing about Miami.*

Now read the next part of Terry's journal.

The real security man from Acme Electronics came about 45 minutes after Ray and Mike left. I think his plane was late, which was why he didn't get here on time. He was friendly at first, but when we told him we didn't have the microfilm, he looked kind of sick. Just then the pizza man came to deliver our pizza. The security man pulled out his gun and opened the door. This scared all of us, including the pizza man, who left as fast as he could. Right after that, Ray called. He said they had followed the guy with the microfilm to a big old house at 367 Mulberry. They thought Tony was tied up inside the house. They were going to sneak in and try to help him. Ray told us to call the police. When I told the security man what Ray had said, he was a little happier. He said he'd call the police and right after that he left.

1. Why does Terry think the security man was late? _____

_____

2. Why was he late? _____

WHAT DO YOU THINK?

Discuss this question in small groups or as a class.

- What do you think Terry, Kim and the security man should do?

THE GANG

At 7:00 that same evening, Tony woke up and found himself tied to a chair in a cold, dark room.

LISTENING WITH A PURPOSE 🔲

Listen to the conversation and look for the answers to these questions.

1. Where is Tony?
2. Why is he tied up?
3. What are Wilbur, Harry and Joe going to do to him?

Do You Know These Words?

buying agent – a person who buys materials, products and equipment for a big company

to feel guilty – to feel you've done something wrong

to commit suicide – to kill yourself

cops – slang for police

LISTENING FOR IMPORTANT DETAILS

Circle the correct answers.

1. Joe kidnapped Tony because
   a. he didn't want Tony to escape.
   b. he wanted Tony to explain the plans.
   c. he wanted Tony's suitcase.

2. Harry and Wilbur have just returned from
   a. taking candy from a baby.   c. Belko Electronics.
   b. the Oregon Hotel.

3. Tony wants
   a. to see the microfilm.   c. to be untied.
   b. to commit suicide.

4. _____ put the microfilm in Tony's suitcase.
   a. Charlie Jackson   c. Terry
   b. Joe

5. The microfilm was put in Tony's suitcase
   a. so he would look like the thief if something went wrong.
   b. because he was going to Washington.
   c. both of the above

6. The microfilm was put in Tony's suitcase
   a. in Miami.   c. at the Oregon Hotel.
   b. at the Washington Airport.

LISTENING FOR LANGUAGE 📼

Listen to the conversation and fill in the blanks.

TONY: It'll never work. My friends can identify you.

HARRY: Well, I have a _____ they're going to have a
                                          1
         little _____ in their hotel room tonight. Right,
                          2
         Joe?

JOE: Right.

WILBUR: Hey, hold on! I didn't know this was _____ to
                                                          3

end up with murder. I was just _____ to save my
                                        4
job. I just wanted to _____ the plans.
                              5
HARRY: Like I _____ before, Wilbur, you're in this just as
                      6
much as we are. So shut _____ or you'll have the
                                   7
same future as the kid here. Now, _____ write
                                            8
that suicide note.

LISTENING FOR ROLES AND RELATIONSHIPS

**Listen to the first conversation again. Write the first letter of
each crook's name next to the description that matches.**

HARRY   WILBUR

JOE   CHARLIE JACKSON

_____ He is guarding Tony.
_____ He took the microfilm
from Tony's friends.
_____ Tony's friends thought
he was the security man
from Acme.
_____ He put the microfilm in
Tony's suitcase.

_____ He is the buying agent
for Belko Electronics.
_____ He parked the car in the
parking garage.
_____ He drove Tony to the
airport.
_____ He doesn't want to kill
anybody.

LISTENING AND FUNCTION PRACTICE

Making comparisons. Harry, one of the crooks, makes comparisons in this episode. He says that getting the film was *"as easy as taking candy from a baby."* This means that taking candy from a baby is easy and getting the film was easy too. He also reminds Wilbur that he is involved in the plan *"just as much as we are."*

Fill in the blanks in the advertisement for the Oregon Hotel. Use the construction:

$$\text{A } is \text{ as} \left\{ \begin{array}{l} \textbf{adjective} \\ \textbf{much/many} \text{ (noun)} \end{array} \right\} as \textbf{ B}$$

THE OREGON HOTEL

Welcome to the Oregon Hotel. We hope your visit here is

_____ pleasant _____ possible. You'll find our serv-
1 2

ice is as _____ as the service in any other hotel in the
3

Washington, D.C. area. Our rates are _____ reasonable
4

_____ in any other hotel in Washington. You'll find our
5

rooms are as _____ as any. We are proud to say the food in
6

our restaurant is as _____ as what you can find in any res-
7

taurant in the city. For one low price you can eat as _____
8

as you want. You can also order as _____ cocktails as you
9

like. We'd like to serve you in any way we can. Please don't hesitate

to offer suggestions.

READING AND LISTENING FOR DIFFERENT POINTS OF VIEW

Read the next part of Terry's journal. Then listen to what is going through Tony's head. What is the difference in their thinking?

After the security man left, Kim and I were really restless. We were worried sick about Tony— and of course about Ray and Mike too. We wished that we had gone with them. They told us all about it later, but it wasn't the same as being there. Apparently this is what happened. Tony finally woke up and then he met his kidnappers. The scar-faced man, whose name was Joe, and Harry, the guy who came to get the microfilm, were both part of the gang. The man who gave us a ride and knocked me down was working with them too, but he wasn't really part of the gang. He was just somebody who worked for an electronics company and was trying to save his job. Anyway, Wilbur, which was this man's name, wasn't really like the others. Harry, the leader, was really ruthless. He had it all arranged for Tony to write a suicide note. He was supposed to feel so bad about stealing the microfilm that he was going to commit suicide.

WHAT DO YOU THINK?

Discuss these in small groups or as a class.

- Describe what happened to Tony from the time he left work until now.
- What do you think will happen to Tony and his friends?

INSIDE THE HOUSE

It's 7:30 P.M. and Ray and Mike are outside the gate trying to attract the dog with Mike's sandwiches.

PREDICTING

Check (√) what you think will happen in this lesson.

____ Mike and Ray will find Tony.

____ Tony will be hurt.

____ Mike and Ray will get hurt.

____ Tony will be rescued by Mike and Ray.

____ The police will come.

____ The men will tie up Mike and Ray.

Listen to the conversation and see if your prediction was correct.

Do You Know These Words?

to close the case – to stop investigating a crime because it is solved

the plug – The end of an electric cord on a lamp which goes into the electric outlet in a wall.

to drown – to die in water

61

LISTENING FOR IMPORTANT DETAILS

Circle *True* or *False*.

1. Mike and Ray go into the house through the front door.   *True*   *False*

2. The crooks want to kill Ray and Mike.   *True*   *False*

3. The crooks are planning to shoot the students.   *True*   *False*

4. Joe and Harry have guns.   *True*   *False*

5. The crooks want to destroy the film.   *True*   *False*

LISTENING FOR LANGUAGE 📼

Listen to the conversation and fill in the blanks.

MIKE: Let's hurry and see if we _____ get inside the
                      1
house before he starts barking again.

RAY: Let's go around to the _____ here. Look. Maybe
                           2
_____ door leads to the basement.
    3

MIKE: It's unlocked.

RAY: There's a light on _____ there. C'mon.
                        4

MIKE: Tony? Is _____ you?
               5

TONY: Ray, Mike! _____ I glad to see you! Untie me.
               6
We've got to get _____ of here fast. _____
               7   8
people are dangerous.

RAY: We can get out the same _____ we came in.
                           9

LISTENING FOR SEQUENCE OF EVENTS 🔲

Listen to the crooks' plan for Tony, Ray and Mike. Reconstruct the plan by filling in the blanks below with your own words.

First, the crooks will make Tony _____ .

Next, the crooks will _____

and put it _____ . Then they

will throw Tony, Mike and Ray _____ .

The police will find _____ with _____

and Mike and Ray _____ .

Finally, the police will _____ .

LISTENING AND FUNCTION PRACTICE

Giving commands. In this episode, direct commands are given because it's a dangerous situation and people have to move quickly.

Untie me!
Hurry!   Pull the plug!
Drop your guns!   Go stand in the corner over there!

In other situations commands are not always so direct. Decide which command form is most appropriate in the following situation and fill in the blanks.

1. TAXI DRIVER: Where do you want to go?

   RAY: _____
                 a. Take me to the Smithsonian Institution!

                 _____
                 b. Take me to the Smithsonian Institution, please.

2. RAY: Mike, those dogs are after us!

   MIKE: _____
                 a. Run! b. Let's run. OK?

3. KIM: Where are the microfilm readers?

   LIBRARIAN: _____
                 a. Follow the signs! b. Just follow the signs.

4. MIKE: Here comes the waitress, Terry.

   TERRY: _____
                 a. Order me a cup of coffee!

                 _____
                 b. Can you order me a cup of coffee, Mike?

READING AND LISTENING FOR SPECIFIC INFORMATION 🔲

Tony's parents called about 9 o'clock to see how the students' vacation was going. Listen to the first part of their conversation and notice that because Terry doesn't want his parents to worry too much, she doesn't tell them everything that has happened. Listen and circle *True* or *False*.

1. Tony's father thinks Tony is a grown man
   who can take care of himself.   *True   False*

2. Tony's mother has more confidence in Tony
   than his father does.   *True   False*

3. Tony's mother is calmer than Tony's father.   *True   False*

Now read Terry's description of the telephone call from Tony's parents.

What happened next was unbelievable. Tony's parents called and wanted to know how we were all doing. They couldn't have called at a worse time!

Mrs. Garcia took the news better than Mr. Garcia did. I told them that Tony felt sick when we landed at the airport, went to get some aspirin and didn't come back. I said that we called the police immediately and they were looking for him, but they hadn't found him. Then Ray and Mike found out where Tony was and we told the police right away. I said that it was really scary for a while, but now it seemed like everything would turn out all right. I didn't say anything about my suitcase or the scar-faced man. I left out the part about Tony being in the basement of that old house because I figured that would make them even more nervous.

According to Terry's journal, which of these sentences might have appeared in the telephone conversation? Check (√) what Terry might have said.

_____ Tony had a headache on the plane.

_____ The police found my suitcase in a trash can at the airport.

_____ Tony disappeared at the airport.

_____ A man has been following us all over Washington.

_____ The police know where Tony is.

_____ Someone broke into my hotel room.

_____ Tony is tied up in the basement of a house.

WHAT DO YOU THINK?

Discuss this question in small groups or as a class.

- What do you think happens after Mike pulls the lamp plug?

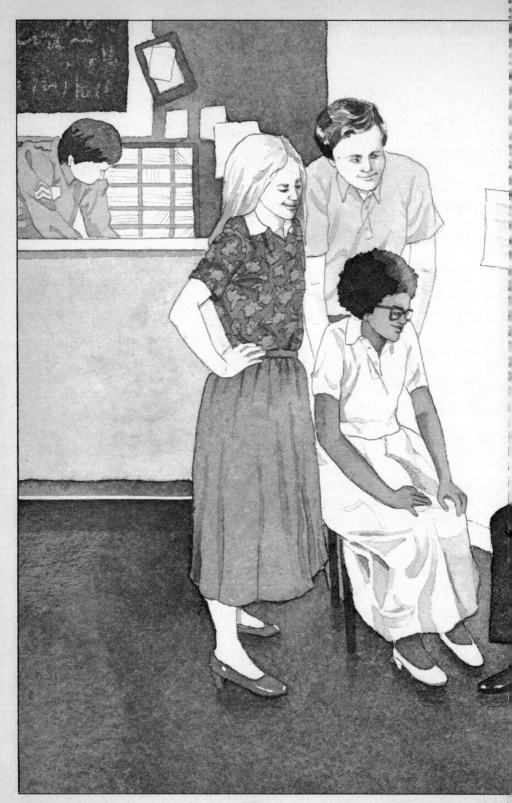

Closing the Case

When the police arrived, the lights went out and. . . .

PREDICTING

What do you think will happen in this episode?

1. What will happen to Tony and his friends?
2. Will anyone get hurt?
3. Will the crooks escape?

Listen to the conversation and see if your prediction is correct.

Do You Know These Words?

to grab – to take with force
to knock out – to hit someone and make him or her lose consciousness
to whisper – to say something very quietly

LISTENING FOR IMPORTANT DETAILS

Circle *True* or *False*.

1. Mike stopped the crooks from escaping by pulling the plug on the lamp. *True* *False*

2. The crooks grabbed Tony at the baggage claim. *True* *False*

3. Charlie Jackson, one of Tony's bosses, was working with the crooks. *True* *False*

4. Charlie Jackson was going to send the plans to Belko Electronics. *True* *False*

5. The students will go out to eat pizza. *True* *False*

LISTENING FOR LANGUAGE 📼

Listen to the conversation and fill in the blanks.

TERRY: Tell us _____(1) happened.

TONY: _____(2) I went to buy some aspirin, a guy grabbed me and stuck a gun in my back. He walked _____(3) to a car and knocked me out. The _____(4) thing I knew, I was tied up in a basement. They _____(5) after the microfilm in my suitcase.

TERRY: _____(6) did they know _____(7) was microfilm in your suitcase?

TONY: Charlie Jackson, one of my bosses at Acme, was secretly _____(8) for a rival company called Belko Electronics. He was supposed to get the plans for _____(9) new battery and send _____(10) to Belko in Washington. _____(11) he found out that

I was going to Washington, he slipped the film in my
suitcase. That way, I _____ get caught instead of
        12
him if anything went wrong.

LISTENING FOR MAIN IDEAS

**What do we know about Charlie Jackson? Check (√) the state-
ments that apply to him.**

_____ He was working for Belko Electronics.

_____ He took Tony to the airport.

_____ He was friendly to Tony.

_____ He was afraid of violence.

_____ He had a more important
job than Tony at Acme.

_____ He knew Harry.

_____ He was married.

_____ He talked to Tony about
his trip to Washington.

_____ He asked Tony to deliver a package for him in Washington.

LISTENING AND FUNCTION PRACTICE

Part 1. *Evaluating what has happened.* **Sometimes we're happy
when someone does something and the results are good. Listen
to Tony and Ray's version of what has happened and complete
their conversation.**

TONY: They were really desperate men. _____

Ray and Mike found me. _____ , I'd be at

the bottom of the Potomac River right now.

RAY: And _____ Kim and Terry called

the police. _____ , we'd be there with you.

Part 2. Use *It's a good thing* and *Otherwise* to express your feelings in these situations.

1. You are walking to school and it starts to rain. A friend stops his car and offers you a ride. You say: _____

_____ . _____ , _____ be soaked.

2. You are in an elevator at work that is stuck between two floors. You don't think anyone will hear you shouting because everyone else has already gone home. But Mr. Jones comes back to get his umbrella, hears you and helps you out. What would you tell him?

_____ .

_____ , _____ still be shouting at the walls.

READING AND LISTENING FOR SPECIFIC INFORMATION

Read the last part of Terry's journal. Look for the answers to these questions and write *True* or *False*.

1. Wilbur was killed in the confusion. _____

2. The gang members were caught because Harry became nervous. _____

3. The students stayed in Washington for a week to finish their vacation. _____

4. Terry is happy about going back to school. _____

About 10 o'clock Detective Sanderson knocked on our hotel room door. By that time Kim and I were worried out of our minds. He told us to come along with him. He took us down to the police station and there we found Ray, Mike and Tony, along with the security man from Acme. They told us the whole story. Pulling the plug on the lamp cord was what saved everybody. When the light went out, Wilbur, who wasn't really a criminal, got scared and tried to run out. On the way out he bumped into Harry. After some moments of shouting and confusion, the police captured everyone. Luckily, no one got hurt. I guess we were really lucky. According to Tony, the crooks were going to kill us all!

After the excitement was over, we went out to a restaurant and celebrated. All of us had steak except for Mike, who had steak and lobster.

This has been an unforgettable vacation. Actually, it's been more like a bad dream than a vacation. I'll be glad to get back to school. We start the day after tomorrow. I'm glad we'll all be there together — Tony and Kim and Mike and Ray.

Now listen to the final conversation with all the friends together at the airport. According to Terry's journal and the conversation, what happened to Harry, Wilbur and Tony after Ray pulled the plug? 🔲

After the lights went out, Wilbur _____ .

He bumped into Harry and _____ .

Tony _____ .

WHAT DO YOU THINK?

Discuss these questions in small groups or as a class.

- What will happen to Charlie Jackson, Joe, Harry and Wilbur?
- How do you think Wilbur feels about what he has done?

LESSON 1

AT THE AIRPORT

Kim, Terry, Mike and Tony are all students at Middletown College in Miami. They decide to visit Washington, D.C. together at the end of their summer vacation. They meet at the baggage claim at Washington National Airport on Friday, August 24.

TERRY: Hello, Kim!

KIM: Hi, Terry. How are you? Did you have a good summer?

TERRY: Yeah, terrific. How about you?

KIM: Yeah, it was great. . . . Terry, I'd like you to meet Ray Lawless. This is Terry Gibson.

RAY: Nice to meet you.

TERRY: Nice to meet you too, Ray. Are you from Quebec City too?

RAY: Yes. Where are you from?

TERRY: Miami.

KIM: Say, where's Mike?

TERRY: At the snack bar, of course.

KIM: Doesn't he ever stop eating?

TERRY: Well, you know Mike.

MIKE: Hi, everybody!

KIM: Hi, Mike.

MIKE: You must be Ray.

RAY: Yeah, I am.

MIKE: Nice to meet you. . . . Well, are we ready to go to the hotel?

KIM: We're still waiting for our luggage and Tony isn't here yet.

MIKE: **Terry, didn't you and Tony fly in together?**

TERRY: **Yes, we did. But when we got off the plane, Tony went to get some aspirin. That was quite a while ago and he still hasn't come back.**

MIKE: **Well, here comes the baggage now.**

TERRY: **Let's get Tony's suitcase for him.**

KIM: **What does it look like?**

TERRY: **It's a small green one, like mine. Look, there it is!**

MIKE: I'll get it.

TERRY: Put it over there with the others. You know, I think we should go look for Tony. Maybe he's sick.

KIM: Where do you think he is?

TERRY: I don't know. But . . . Hey! That man is walking away with Tony's suitcase! Stop him! He's running away! Stop him!

RAY: Stop!

MIKE: I don't think Ray can catch him in this crowd.

KIM: Why would anybody want to steal Tony's suitcase?

TERRY: Good question. Where *is* Tony anyway?

LISTENING FOR LANGUAGE
Listen to the conversation and fill in the blanks.

For text of practice, see boldface section of previous dialog.

READING AND LISTENING FOR SPECIFIC INFORMATION

Listen to the conversation between Mike and a policeman and circle the correct answer.

MIKE: Excuse me. Can you help me?

POLICEMAN: Sure, what's your problem?

MIKE: A group of us are on a trip together and we have a friend who was going to meet us here. He went to get something to eat and he didn't come back. That was a while ago. We think he might be in trouble. Also, a man ran away with his suitcase, at least I think it was his suitcase. What can we do?

POLICEMAN: These things happen all the time. Your friend probably ran into someone he knew. We can't do anything unless he's really missing. Wait till morning—if he hasn't turned up by then, you can go to the station and fill out a missing persons report. As for the suitcase, maybe it belonged to the guy who took it and he was just in a hurry. A lot of suitcases look alike.

MIKE: You mean there's nothing we can do now to find him?

POLICEMAN: No, not now. Wait till morning.

LESSON 2

THE OREGON HOTEL

It's 5:00 P.M. and the students are still at the airport. Mike has just talked to the police about Tony and the stolen suitcase.

RAY: What did the police say, Mike?

MIKE: They said they couldn't do anything because the suitcase might belong to the man who picked it up.

RAY: What? That's ridiculous.

MIKE: They also said that we have to come to the station to fill out a report on Tony.

STRANGER: Excuse me. I couldn't help overhearing your conversation. Are you having some trouble?

TERRY: We sure are! A friend of ours disappeared from this airport an hour ago and now somebody has stolen his suitcase.

STRANGER: Maybe that wasn't his suitcase after all. Maybe he's already picked up his suitcase and gone to the hotel.

TERRY: No. Tony wouldn't do that. We were all supposed to meet here at the baggage claim.

STRANGER: Where are you staying?

RAY: At the Oregon Hotel.

STRANGER: I bet he's there. Why don't you let me give you a ride? I'm going that way.

KIM: Thanks, but we can get a taxi.

STRANGER: A taxi? Oh no, I insist. I have a son just about your age and I'd like to help out if I can.

MIKE: What do you think?

RAY: Maybe he's right. Maybe we should go to the hotel. At least Tony could call us there.

STRANGER: OK, come on then. My car's right outside.

Here you are—The Oregon Hotel. Let me help you with your suitcases.

I'll just put your suitcases down here next to the reservation desk.

MIKE: Thanks a lot.

CLERK: May I help you?

RAY: We have reservations for two rooms, under *Ray Lawless*.

CLERK: Oh yes ... a reservation for five. Sign here, please.

RAY: Has Tony Garcia checked in yet? He's one of our group.

CLERK: No, he isn't here yet. Here are your keys.

RAY: Thank you.

MIKE: Why don't I call the airport and have Tony paged again while you put our stuff up in the rooms? Then I'll meet you in the restaurant. I'm starving.

TERRY: **Hey, what happened to that man who gave us a ride?**

KIM: **I don't know. I guess he left.**

TERRY: **We didn't even get a chance to thank him.**

RAY: **That's too bad. Did anyone get his name?**

MIKE: **No, he never mentioned it. And he left without saying goodbye.**

RAY: **You're right. How strange.**

LISTENING FOR LANGUAGE

Listen to the conversation and fill in the blanks.

See boldface section of previous dialog.

READING AND LISTENING FOR DIFFERENT POINTS OF VIEW

Listen to the conversation between Kim and Ray about someone they met at the airport.

KIM: Ray, don't you think it's a little strange that that man just appeared all of a sudden?

RAY: Well, I guess so, but he seemed like a really nice person.

KIM: Why do you think he wanted to help us?

RAY: Well, he said he had a son about our age.

KIM: Sure, but lots of people have kids our age and they still don't give rides to people they don't know.

RAY: What are you saying? Do you think he had anything to do with Tony's disappearance?

KIM: I don't know. Maybe. I just think the whole thing is hard to believe. Also, he was listening to our conversation. How many people actually listen very much to what other people say?

RAY: I think you're worrying too much. He's just a nice, helpful man. Be glad there are people like him around.

LESSON 3

DINNER TIME

By 6:00 P.M. the students have checked into the hotel. They decide to get something to eat while they're waiting to hear from Tony.

MIKE: I'm hungry. Let's order.

KIM: You're always hungry, Mike. Did you have any luck paging Tony?

MIKE: No luck. He must not be anywhere in the airport.

P.A.: Telephone call for Terry Gibson. Terry Gibson, telephone, please.

RAY: Terry, that's for you!

TERRY: Maybe it's Tony.

KIM: Do you think that Tony could be at the airport looking for his suitcase?

MIKE: I already thought of that. I called the Lost Baggage Office, but he hasn't been there.

WAITRESS: **Are you ready to order?**

MIKE: **Yes! I want two cheeseburgers with ketchup, onions and pickles, fries, onion rings and a chocolate milkshake, please.**

RAY: **Mike, how can you eat so much and stay so thin? I think I'll just have an egg salad sandwich and some black coffee.**

KIM: **I'd like the fried chicken dinner with mashed potatoes and gravy, a piece of cheesecake and a diet cola.**

WAITRESS: **Is that all?**

RAY: Our friend is on the phone. Could you come back to get her order in a few minutes?

WAITRESS: OK.

MIKE: **I'm worried about Tony. Maybe he really got sick.**

KIM: **Yeah, maybe we should check the hospitals. Terry said he felt bad on the plane. He had a sore throat and was really tired.**

MIKE: **I can see why. He works twenty hours a week at Acme and you know how much he studies. I don't know how he does it.**

RAY: **Here comes Terry.**

KIM: **Who was on the phone?**

TERRY: **The police! They found my suitcase in a trash can at the airport!**

RAY: How did they know where to call you?

TERRY: I had the hotel confirmation slip in my suitcase.

KIM: Then whose suitcase do we have in our room?

RAY: Good question! Let's go find out!

LISTENING FOR LANGUAGE

Listen to the conversation and fill in the blanks.
See second boldface section of previous dialog.

INTENSIVE LISTENING

Listen to what the students order at the restaurant and match the person to the order.
See first boldface section of previous dialog.

READING AND LISTENING FOR DIFFERENT POINTS OF VIEW

Listen to the conversation and answer this question.

TERRY: Hello?

DETECTIVE: Is this Terry Gibson?

TERRY: Yes, it is.

DETECTIVE: This is Detective Sanderson at the Washington Police Department. Ms. Gibson, may I ask what you're doing in Washington?

TERRY: What I'm doing here? What do you mean?

DETECTIVE: Why are you in Washington? Do you have business here?

TERRY: I'm with friends. We're sightseeing before we go back to school. Why?

DETECTIVE: Do you know why your suitcase was in a trash can at the airport?

TERRY: My suitcase? I'm sorry, Mr. Sanderson, but I don't know what you're talking about.

DETECTIVE: Ms. Gibson, we found your suitcase in a trash can. There were a few articles of clothing in it. That's all. People don't go around dropping their luggage in the trash. What was in the suitcase?

TERRY: Mr. Sanderson, I picked up my suitcase at the airport this afternoon. Why do you think the suitcase you found is mine?

DETECTIVE: Because your hotel confirmation slip was in it.

TERRY: Then whose suitcase do I have?

DETECTIVE: I don't know, Ms. Gibson.

LESSON 4

AN INTRUDER

Terry receives a phone call from the police. The students rush up to her room to see whose suitcase is there.

MIKE: Here we are, fifth floor.

TERRY: I can't believe I have the wrong suitcase.

KIM: I don't understand why anyone would put your suitcase in a trash can.

RAY: Here's your room. . . . Your door is open.

KIM: That's funny. I remember locking it.

TERRY: **There's a man in here! Hey, who are you? What are you doing with that suitcase?**

MIKE: **Hey you! Come back here! Come on, Ray, let's see if we can catch him.**

KIM: **Terry, are you all right?**

TERRY: **Oh, my head!**

KIM: **Here, let me help you up.**

MIKE: It's no use. He got on the elevator and the door closed before we got there.

RAY: Terry . . . if he hurt you, I'll. . . .

TERRY: I'm all right. I just hit my head when he knocked me down.

MIKE: At least he didn't get away with the suitcase.

KIM: That's right—the suitcase! Let's see whose it is.

MIKE: If it isn't yours, Terry, how come it has your initials on it? See here? T.G.

EVERYBODY: Tony Garcia!

KIM: Open it, Mike!

MIKE: Yup. This is Tony's suitcase all right. Here's his red jacket.

KIM: Let's see what else is in it.

MIKE: What's in this big envelope? Hmm—what's this?

KIM: Let's see. It's microfilm! Let me hold it up to the light. I'm not sure, but it looks like blueprints.

MIKE: What's Tony doing with blueprints?

RAY: Is this what that man was looking for?

TERRY: Uh-oh! I hope he doesn't come back!

RAY: You know, I couldn't tell for sure, but he looked a lot like the guy who brought us to the hotel this afternoon.

KIM: You're right. He did! Maybe that explains why he was so friendly and then left without saying goodbye.

MIKE: You mean he was just interested in stealing this suitcase?

TERRY: We'd better call the police!

KIM: OK, but let's not say anything about the microfilm yet. Let's see what's on it first.

LISTENING FOR LANGUAGE

Listen to the conversation and fill in the blanks.

See boldface section of previous dialog.

READING AND LISTENING FOR SPECIFIC INFORMATION

Listen to the conversation between Wilbur and Joe and answer the questions.

JOE: Hello.

WILBUR: Joe, this is Wilbur. We've got a problem.

JOE: Why? What have you messed up now?

WILBUR: Listen, it wasn't my fault. I gave the kids a ride to their hotel. I waited while they got settled. Then they went to the restaurant to eat dinner. I thought they'd be gone quite a while, so I didn't hurry. I was going through the suitcase and I saw the envelope the microfilm was in, but right then I heard them coming. I just had time to get out of the room and I had to knock one of the girls down. The boys chased me and almost caught me. I tell you, Joe, I'm not a criminal. All I'm worried about is my job. I don't like all this violence.

JOE: Now listen, Wilbur, and get this straight. You're in this as much as we are. Do this right or else you're going to end up like the kids. I'll be at the hotel in the morning. You do what I told you before.

LESSON 5

THE PLANS

At 9:00 the next morning, the students take the microfilm to a nearby library. They want to use one of the microfilm machines to find out what is on the film.

MIKE: Boy, the police haven't been very helpful, have they?

TERRY: You can say that again. They seem to believe that since we have Tony's suitcase, he'll turn up eventually.

KIM: Well, I'll feel better when we find out what's on this microfilm. Here's the library.

TERRY: Don't forget. As soon as we finish here, we have to go to the police station to pick up my suitcase.

RAY: The microfilm reading machines are over there.

KIM: **Mike, you *did* bring the microfilm, didn't you?**

MIKE: **Of course! I have it right here. How does this stupid machine work? I can't get the microfilm to go in.**

KIM: **Here, let me show you. It's easy. You do it like this.**

MIKE: **Will you look at this! Why in the world did Tony have something like this in his suitcase?**

TERRY: **Let me look. Good grief! What is that stuff? I can't make heads or tails of it.**

KIM: **Those are diagrams and chemical formulas for some kind of battery.**

TERRY: **How can you tell?**

KIM: **We studied different kinds of batteries in chemical engineering last semester.**

MIKE: Well, I don't see why anyone would break into your room just to get the plans for some stupid battery.

KIM: That depends on the battery. Look at this part, Mike. This is incredible. It looks like it's a battery for an electric car.

MIKE: An electric car?

KIM: Yeah. According to these figures, this battery would be cheap to produce and a car could go for 500 miles at 55 m.p.h. before you would have to re-charge it.

MIKE: Then people wouldn't need gasoline or gas powered cars anymore, would they?

KIM: No, they wouldn't. Now you see why that man is trying to get it.

RAY: I wonder why this was in Tony's suitcase.

KIM: I don't know. Let's see if we can find a name somewhere. There.... Do you see it?

MIKE: Yes, it looks like Acme ... Acme Electronics Corporation. That's the company Tony works for!

KIM: Do you think that they asked him to deliver the film to someone while he was here in Washington?

MIKE: I don't think so. After all, Tony's just an office boy.

KIM: I think we should call the company and find out what's going on. I feel certain that Tony's disappearance has something to do with this film.

LISTENING FOR LANGUAGE

Listen to the conversation and then fill in the blanks.
See boldface section of previous dialog.

READING AND LISTENING FOR DIFFERENT POINTS OF VIEW

Listen to the conversation between Kim and Mike.

KIM: Mike, what do you think about all this? You don't think Tony stole the microfilm, do you?

MIKE: I sure don't. Tony wouldn't do a thing like that.

KIM: What makes you so sure?

MIKE: I've known Tony since we were kids. He's almost too honest. One time in sixth grade everyone was cheating on an exam, but Tony wouldn't cheat.

KIM: That's what I thought. I just wanted to hear it from you. But what do you think happened?

MIKE: I think Tony did go and buy some aspirin, but somebody picked him up at the drugstore.

KIM: How would they know when he was coming in?

MIKE: Maybe they were on the plane he and Terry were on. They just followed him when he got off.

KIM: Who do you think these people are?

MIKE: I'm not sure, but they might be industrial spies.

LESSON 6

ACME

The students have discovered that the microfilm contains plans from Acme Corporation, the company that Tony works for. They call Miami and speak to Dr. Franklin, head of the Acme research department.

KIM: Yes, I think the plans are for some kind of battery.

DR. FRANKLIN: I don't understand what you're doing with them.

KIM: Our friend Tony Garcia works for your company. He disappeared at the airport yesterday and we have no idea where he is. We found the plans in his suitcase last night.

DR. FRANKLIN: In his suitcase! Where are the plans now?

KIM: I have them with me.

DR. FRANKLIN: Where are you staying?

KIM: At the Oregon Hotel, on K Street.

DR. FRANKLIN: Kim, we do have top-secret plans for a battery. Look, I'll send a security man to pick up the film right away. He should be at your hotel in the late afternoon.

KIM: OK. Thank you, Dr. Franklin.

DR. FRANKLIN: Thank you for calling.

RAY: Well, what did you find out? Did she say anything about Tony?

KIM: No, not really.

MIKE: Poor Tony. I wish we knew where he was.

KIM: All we can do is wait and talk to the security man. He might have some information for us.

RAY: What can we do until then?

MIKE: Let's get something to eat. I'm starved.

KIM: That's a good idea, but we really should go back to the hotel. We can eat there.

TERRY: OK. Let's go. But remember, after lunch we have to go pick up my suitcase—or what's left of it.

MIKE: On our way back, let's walk up Constitution Avenue. Maybe we can at least see a few things.

RAY: There's the Lincoln Memorial. And look over there. Isn't that pool beautiful?

KIM: According to the map it's the Reflecting Pond.

TERRY: And the Washington Monument is at the other end.

MIKE: What's that old reddish-colored building across the Mall? It looks like a castle.

KIM: I think it's the Smithsonian Institution. Wait a minute. . . . Look at that man over there.

TERRY: Which man?

KIM: The one with a scar on his face. I think he's following us.

RAY: Really?

KIM: Yes. I saw him at the hotel and again at the library, and now he's right behind us.

TERRY: I know who he is. He's the man who ran off with my suitcase.

MIKE: Do you think he's after the microfilm?

RAY: Probably. There's a taxi. Let's see if we can lose him.

LISTENING FOR LANGUAGE

Listen to the conversation and fill in the blanks.

See boldface section of previous dialog.

READING AND LISTENING FOR SPECIFIC INFORMATION

Listen to the conversation between Dr. Franklin and the security man who is going to pick up the microfilm.

DR. FRANKLIN: Jim, we've got a serious problem. I want you to go to Washington and pick up some microfilm.

SECURITY MAN: What's this all about?

DR. FRANKLIN: I just got a call from some kids in Washington. It seems they found a film of our plan for the new battery in one of their suitcases.

SECURITY MAN: What? How did that happen? Who are these kids?

DR. FRANKLIN: Do you know Tony Garcia? These kids are friends of his. They're all in Washington on a trip together and the microfilm turned up in his suitcase.

SECURITY MAN: Who's Tony Garcia?

DR. FRANKLIN: He's an office boy here.

SECURITY MAN: What kind of record does he have?

DR. FRANKLIN: I've heard nothing but good things about him, but I think we have to assume he's in on this.

SECURITY MAN: You don't think somebody else took the film? One of the scientists, maybe?

DR. FRANKLIN: No, I don't, Jim. I think we can trust all of the researchers here.

SECURITY MAN: OK. When do I leave?

FRANKLIN: Right away. You're on the 12 o'clock plane to Washington. Another thing: I told the girl I talked to that we have plans for the battery. I really shouldn't have said that. Do you think there's anything we can do about it?

SECURITY MAN: Not too much, but I'll tell them not to say anything to anybody.

LESSON 7

THE PICKUP

After returning from the library, the students ate lunch at the hotel and then Terry and Ray went to the station to pick up her suitcase. By 6:00 P.M., they were all back at the hotel and Mike was hungry again.

MIKE: Look, since we have to wait here for the security man, why don't we order a pizza? I'm so hungry I can't think straight.

KIM: That's not a bad idea. Here's the phone book.

MIKE: OK. Let's see now. Hmm. Here's a place that delivers. Should we get a medium or a large?

RAY: The way you eat, I think we should get an extra large.

MIKE: OK.

PIZZA MAN: Dino's Pizza.

MIKE: I'd like to order an extra large pizza, please, with mushrooms and pepperoni.

PIZZA MAN: OK. I need your name, address and phone number.

MIKE: Mike Capra, C-A-P-R-A. The Oregon Hotel, 233 K Street, Room 524. The phone number is 572-6684.

PIZZA MAN: OK. We'll have it there in 45 minutes.

MIKE: Thanks.

TERRY: I don't think I can eat any pizza right now.

RAY: Terry, do you feel all right?

TERRY: All this excitement has given me a terrible headache.

MIKE: I'll get it. Are you the security man from the Acme Electronics Corporation?

MAN: Uh, yeah. That's right.

MIKE: Boy, are we glad to see you. You got here pretty fast.

MAN: Well, we wanted to get that film back as quickly as possible.

RAY: It sure has caused us a lot of trouble.

MAN: Yeah, well, your troubles are over now.

RAY: Say, have you found out anything about our friend Tony?

MAN: Well . . . uh . . . no, but we'll get in touch with you as soon as we find out anything.

KIM: Thanks for picking up the microfilm.

MAN: OK. See you later.

TERRY: I'm so glad to get rid of that microfilm.

RAY: Now all we have to worry about is where Tony is.

KIM: Hello? Oh, Dr. Franklin. What? Oh no! Mike, Ray, Dr. Franklin is calling to say the security man won't be here for another half hour.

RAY: Then who was that man who was just here?

KIM: I don't know.

MIKE: Don't worry. We'll stop him. C'mon, Ray, let's go.

LISTENING FOR LANGUAGE

Listen to the conversation and fill in the blanks.

See boldface section of previous dialog.

READING AND LISTENING FOR SPECIFIC INFORMATION

Earlier that afternoon Joe, the scar-faced man, called Harry, one of the gang members. Listen to their conversation and fill in the blanks.

HARRY: Hello?

JOE: Harry?

HARRY: Yeah, this is Harry. Where are you now?

JOE: I'm at the coffee shop across from the hotel where the kids are staying. I followed them to the library this morning. They put the microfilm on a machine, so they know what's on it for sure. I followed them outside and they jumped in a taxi. They thought they lost me. Dumb kids.

HARRY: Yeah, that's what I figured. Now, listen. Charlie Jackson has a tap on Franklin's phone. The kids called her and told her the whole story, so now we've got to move fast. Franklin is sending a security man to pick up the film late in the afternoon. I'm going to do what I can to keep him from getting it.

JOE: What are you going to do?

HARRY: Don't worry about it. We have a special cab driver who takes care of these things.

JOE: You're not going to kill him, are you? We don't need that.

HARRY: Shut up and quit asking questions. I'll take care of him. Now get over to Mulberry.

LESSON 8

A WILD CHASE

Ray and Mike rush out of the hotel and see the man who took the microfilm going by in a black Chevy. They get a cab and follow him to the other side of town.

MIKE: This is good. We'll get out here.

CAB DRIVER: That'll be $11.50.

MIKE: Wow! Well, all right. Here you go. Keep the change. . . . **Ray, where are we?**

RAY: **Don't worry. While you were helping the cab driver follow the car, I was watching where we were going.**

MIKE: **We're quite a way from the hotel, aren't we?**

RAY: **We sure are. The guy parked the car over there. Did you see where he went after he got out?**

MIKE: **Yeah, he went into that old house.**

RAY: **The one with the brick wall around it?**

MIKE: **Yeah.**

RAY: **OK. Let's go.**

MIKE: **Are you crazy?**

RAY: They have the microfilm in there.

MIKE: Yeah, and they could have guns, too!

RAY: C'mon, we'll be careful.

MIKE: How will we get over this wall?

RAY: Let's try the iron gate. Look, it's open.

MIKE: Shhh! We don't want anyone to hear us.

RAY: There's light coming from that basement window. Let's go take a look.

MIKE: Can you see anything?

RAY: Yes. It looks like someone is tied up in there.

MIKE: Let me see. Hey, that looks like Tony! This window is so dirty I can't tell for sure.

RAY: What's that noise?

MIKE: Uh-oh. It sounds like a dog barking.

RAY: You're right. **What a funny-looking dog.**

MIKE: **I've never seen such big ears. And look at those teeth.**

RAY: **Wow! And look, they must have cut off its tail.**

MIKE: **Those spots are really strange too. Hey, he's coming after us! Let's get out of here!**

RAY: **Hurry. . . . We'll have to get back through the gate. Hurry up, Mike!**

MIKE: Whew! That was close.

RAY: Now, how are we going to get inside the house?

MIKE: Inside the house? What do we want to do that for?

RAY: If Tony's in there, we've got to help him.

MIKE: How?

RAY: I don't know. Let me think about it for a minute.

MIKE: Well, while you're thinking, I'm going to have one of these sandwiches I brought along. I didn't get a chance to eat them all.

RAY: That's it!

MIKE: What?

RAY: Give me those sandwiches. We'll distract the dog with them and get into the house.

MIKE: Well, it might work. First, we'd better call Kim and Terry and tell them to call the police.

RAY: Good idea. I think I see a phone booth down the street.

LISTENING FOR LANGUAGE

Listen to the conversation and fill in the blanks.

See boldface section of previous dialog.

LISTENING FOR DETAILS

Listen to Ray and Mike's description of the dog. Which drawing best matches their description?

See boldface section of previous dialog.

READING AND LISTENING FOR DIFFERENT POINTS OF VIEW

Mike and Ray are in a taxi following the man who has the microfilm. Listen to their conversation and circle *True* or *False*.

RAY: How long have you known Terry?

MIKE: Quite a while. I met her the first semester we were in college, at a Halloween party.

RAY: Did you ever go out with her?

MIKE: Sure, a lot. We really had quite a romance for a while.

RAY: So, what happened?

MIKE: Oh, we both started getting involved in other things. I was on the tennis team and was really busy. And then we started going out with other people. We're just friends now.

RAY: What about Tony? Didn't they come here together?

MIKE: Yeah, but that was just because they got a later flight. He has a girlfriend back at school.

RAY: Does Terry have a boyfriend?

MIKE: Nobody serious right now. Say, why all the questions? Are you interested?

RAY: I don't know. Maybe.

LESSON 9
BACK AT THE HOTEL

It's 7:00 P.M. and Terry and Kim are waiting for the real security man from Acme.

TERRY: Oh, how could we be so stupid! I don't believe we gave the microfilm to the wrong man.

KIM: I guess we were in too much of a hurry to get rid of it.

TERRY: Yes?

SECURITY MAN: Hello. I'm from Acme Electronics.

KIM: Oh, am I glad to see you!

SECURITY MAN: I came to pick up the microfilm.

TERRY: Well, we don't actually have it.

SECURITY MAN: What do you mean you don't have it?

KIM: What she means is we accidentally gave it to the wrong person. A man came to our door a little while ago. We thought he was from Acme, so we gave him the microfilm.

SECURITY MAN: What did he look like?

KIM: He was tall and blond—

TERRY: And he was wearing a dark suit.

SECURITY MAN: Are you expecting anyone?

KIM: No.

SECURITY MAN: Then let me answer the door.

SECURITY MAN: Yes?

TERRY: Oh my gosh, Kim, he has a gun!

PIZZA MAN: Take it easy. I'm just delivering your pizza.

KIM: Oh, that's right. I forgot about the pizza.

PIZZA MAN: Look, I just want $8.75 and then I'll get out of here.

TERRY: Here you are—$8.75.

SECURITY MAN: You know, if you're trying to help Tony get away with that microfilm, you're going to be in a lot of trouble.

TERRY: We're not! We don't even know where Tony is right now.

KIM: **I'll get it. Hello? . . . Ray! Where are you? . . . Did you find out anything? . . . Where is he? . . . Just a minute. Let me get a pencil. . . . OK. I'm ready. . . . Got it. . . . Ray, I don't think that's a good idea. Why don't you call—Darn! He hung up.**

SECURITY MAN: Who was that?

KIM: Our friends, Ray and Mike. They followed the man with the microfilm.

SECURITY MAN: Where are they now?

KIM: At a phone booth near 367 Mulberry, wherever that is. The man went into the house, so Ray and Mike looked inside and they saw someone tied up in the basement. They think it's Tony.

TERRY: Really? Oh, I hope Tony's all right.

KIM: I'm not only worried about Tony. Ray said he and Mike were going to try to sneak inside. Those men could be dangerous!

SECURITY MAN: And those men supposedly have the microfilm?

KIM: Yes. We've got to do something.

LISTENING FOR LANGUAGE

Listen to the conversation and fill in the blanks.

See boldface section of previous dialog.

LISTENING AND MAKING INFERENCES

Listen to Kim and Ray's telephone conversation. Fill in Ray's part of the conversation.

See boldface section of previous dialog.

READING AND LISTENING FOR SPECIFIC INFORMATION

Listen to the conversation between the security man and a cab driver who picks him up at the airport.

WHITESIDE: Taxi!
The Oregon Hotel. It's on K Street.

DRIVER: We might have a little trouble getting there. The freeway is closed because of construction, but I'll get you there as soon as I can.

WHITESIDE: Yes, please do. I'm in a hurry.

DRIVER: Where are you from?

WHITESIDE: Miami.

DRIVER: Oh, I know Miami. I have an aunt who lives there. It's a great place.

WHITESIDE: Yes. Uh, can you drive a little faster, please? As I said, I'm in a hurry.

DRIVER: Of course. And that new amusement park they're constructing— Have you seen it?

WHITESIDE: No, I haven't. Can't you go a little faster?

DRIVER: The speed limit is 45. I don't want a ticket.

WHITESIDE: I think we're on the wrong road. We should be taking M Street to get to the hotel.

DRIVER: No, they've made M Street a one-way street in the other direction. We're OK.

WHITESIDE: This is ridiculous. You drive slower than my grandmother and we're going around in circles. I'm getting out of this car.

DRIVER: OK. It's up to you. That'll be $10.30.

LESSON 10

THE GANG

At 7:00 that same evening, Tony woke up and found himself tied to a chair in a cold, dark room.

TONY: Oh, my head. Where am I? Who are you? What am I doing here?

JOE: It's about time you woke up.

TONY: Why am I tied to this chair? These ropes are hurting my arms.

JOE: Oh, shut up, kid.

TONY: Can't you take these off? They're really hurting me.

JOE: Sorry, but I wouldn't want you to get any ideas about trying to get out of here.

TONY: Why did you bring me here? What do you want from me?

JOE: It isn't you we want. It's your suitcase. We couldn't let you go to the baggage claim and cause any trouble, could we?

TONY: My suitcase? What would you want with my suitcase? There was nothing really valuable in it.

JOE: Hey, Harry, Wilbur. Did you get the film?

HARRY: I sure did, Joe. It was as easy as taking candy from a baby. Those dumb kids thought I was the security man from Acme.

JOE: Good job, Harry!

HARRY: Yes, but no thanks to Wilbur here. He almost messed the whole thing up. I told him to wait out front in the car. When I came back, he wasn't there. I finally found him parked in the garage.

WILBUR: Well, I'm not used to doing this kind of thing.

HARRY: I know, I know, you're just a buying agent from Belko Electronics. Well, you'd better get used to it. If anything goes wrong, you're in this just as much as we are.

JOE: What about the kid here?

HARRY: He's going to feel so guilty about stealing the microfilm that he's going to commit suicide!

TONY: Hey, wait a minute! I didn't steal anything!

HARRY: After you write the suicide note, everyone will think you did. We don't want the cops to figure out that Charlie Jackson got that microfilm for us.

TONY: Charlie Jackson! Oh, now I see. I was really happy when Charlie offered to take me to the airport. He just wanted to put the microfilm in my suitcase. That's why you wanted my suitcase, right?

HARRY: You're a smart kid. When Charlie heard that you were leaving for Washington, he knew he could slip the microfilm into your suitcase. If anything went wrong, it would look like you were the thief.

TONY: It'll never work. My friends can identify you.

HARRY: Well, I have a feeling they're going to have a little accident in their hotel room tonight. Right, Joe?

JOE: Right.

WILBUR: Hey, hold on! I didn't know this was going to end up with murder. I was just trying to save my job. I — I just wanted to get the plans.

HARRY: Like I said before, Wilbur, you're in this just as much as we are. So shut up or you'll have the same future as the kid here. Now, let's write that suicide note.

LISTENING FOR LANGUAGE

Listen to the conversation and fill in the blanks.

See boldface section of previous dialog.

READING AND LISTENING FOR DIFFERENT POINTS OF VIEW

Listen to what is going through Tony's head.

What am I going to do now? What are

they going to do to me? Boy, if I ever get out of this alive, I'm going to see that the police catch these guys and I'm going to make sure Charlie Jackson gets sent to jail. What a terrible guy. I always thought he was a nice person. I always thought he liked me.

I used to complain about having so much to do—about school and work and never getting enough sleep, but all that looks pretty good right now. I wonder what Terry and Kim and Mike and that other guy—what was his name? Ray, I guess. I wonder what they're all doing right now. They're probably out having a great time. They probably just think I ran into somebody I knew. I wonder if I'll ever see them again.

I wonder ... that Wilbur doesn't seem like such a bad guy. He said he didn't want to be involved in murder. Maybe I could persuade him to help me escape. I could offer to pay him. I'll wait until Harry and Joe leave the room and just Wilbur is here. Harry and Joe are out of this room a lot. We'd probably have time to escape before they came back.

LESSON 11
INSIDE THE HOUSE

It's 7:30 P.M. and Ray and Mike are outside the gate trying to attract the dog with Mike's sandwiches.

RAY: Once the dog comes after the sandwiches, throw them over by that tree so we have time to get in the gate.

MIKE: Here fella. How about a sandwich? Nice boy. Go get 'em!

RAY: Quick, inside the gate.

MIKE: **Let's hurry and see if we can get inside the house before he starts barking again.**

RAY: **Let's go around to the back here. Look. Maybe that door leads to the basement.**

MIKE: **It's unlocked.**

RAY: **There's a light on down there. C'mon.**

MIKE: **Tony? Is that you?**

TONY: **Ray, Mike! Am I glad to see you! Untie me. We've got to get out of here fast. These people are dangerous.**

RAY: **We can get out the same way we came in.**

TONY: **I hear someone coming. Hurry!**

JOE: **Well, well, who do we have here? Not so fast. Go stand in the corner over there. So your friends came to help you, huh, kid? Harry! Wilbur! Come on down here and see what I've found.**

HARRY: Well. Some visitors came to see us.

MIKE: We ... we were just. . . .

JOE: Shut up! What should we do with them?

RAY: We won't cause any trouble. We promise not to say anything.

HARRY: It's too late for that. Before you called Acme, they didn't even know the microfilm was missing. Now they know someone has stolen their plans, so we've got to give them a thief.

JOE: **Tony, here, is going to write a suicide note saying he stole the film. He feels so bad that he's taking it with him to the bottom of the river.**

HARRY: **Right. We'll make a copy of this film and when the police find Tony in the river with the film in his pocket, they'll close the case.**

JOE: **But what about these two, Harry?**

HARRY: **I guess they'll just have to drown, trying to save their friend.**

POLICE: Drop your guns. This is the police.

HARRY: Drop *your* guns or this kid will have a bullet through his head!

RAY: Mike, pull the plug on the lamp.

LISTENING FOR LANGUAGE

Listen to the conversation and fill in the blanks.

See boldface section of previous dialog.

LISTENING FOR SEQUENCE OF EVENTS

Listen to the crooks' plan for Tony, Ray and Mike.

See boldface section of previous dialog.

READING AND LISTENING FOR SPECIFIC INFORMATION

Tony's parents called about 9 o'clock to see how the students' vacation was going. Listen to the first part of their conversation and notice that because Terry doesn't want his parents to worry too much, she doesn't tell them everything that has happened.

TERRY: Hello?

MRS. GARCIA: Hello. Terry is that you? This is Mrs. Garcia.

TERRY: Oh, hi.

MR. GARCIA: Hi, Terry.

TERRY: Hi, Mr. Garcia.

MRS. GARCIA: We called to see how you kids are doing in Washington. I bet you're all having a great time!

TERRY: Well, uh . . .

MRS. GARCIA: Is Tony there? We called his room, but there wasn't any answer.

TERRY: It's great of you to call . . . uh . . . no, Tony isn't here right now.

MR. GARCIA: He's probably out somewhere, huh?

TERRY: Uh, no, not really. No, uh, Mr. Garcia . . . there's a little problem.

MR. GARCIA: A little problem? What kind of problem?

TERRY: Well, we don't really know where Tony is right now. You see, when we landed at—

MR. GARCIA: What? You don't know where he is? I knew it, I knew it. Something's happened to that boy.

MRS. GARCIA: Now Hector, calm down. Give Terry a chance to tell us what happened.

TERRY: Well, we landed at the airport and Tony had a headache, so he went to get . . . uh . . . he went to get some aspirin, but then we couldn't find him and—

MR. GARCIA: Couldn't find him? What? You mean he's missing? He's a missing person? Have you called the police? Have you called the FBI? Helen, I knew we never should have let that boy go on this trip. I told you he'd—

MRS. GARCIA: Hector, calm down! He's a responsible young man. Now, Terry, what actually happened?

TERRY: Well, like I said, he didn't come back. We told the police about it and they're looking for him. In fact, they think they know where he is. They think he's at a house on Mulberry Street.

LESSON 12

CLOSING THE CASE

When the police arrived, the lights went out and . . .

POLICE: All right you guys! Up against the wall! Are you kids OK? It's a good thing you unplugged the lamp. That was fast thinking.

RAY: Boy, are we glad you came!

POLICE: You're lucky we did. Come on, let's go down to the station so we can fill out a report on these guys.

TERRY: Tony! Are we glad to see you. **Tell us what happened.**

TONY: **When I went to buy some as-** **pirin, a guy grabbed me and stuck a gun in my back. He walked me to a car and knocked me out. The next thing I knew, I was tied up in a basement. They were after the microfilm in my suitcase.**

TERRY: **How did they know there was microfilm in your suitcase?**

TONY: **Charlie Jackson, one of my bosses at Acme, was secretly working for a rival company called Belko**

Electronics. He was supposed to get the plans for our new battery and send them to Belko in Washington. When he found out that I was going to Washington, he slipped the film in my suitcase. That way, I would get caught instead of him if anything went wrong.

KIM: Did Ray and Mike ever get into the house?

TONY: Oh yes. Those crooks were planning to kill me when Mike and Ray broke in. We tried to escape, but they caught us. I was sure they were going to kill us all until the police got there.

MIKE: Then one of the crooks grabbed Tony and put a gun to his head.

TERRY: Oh no! How did you get away?

MIKE: Ray whispered to me to pull the plug on the lamp. When the lights went out, Wilbur, who really wasn't a crook, got scared and ran out. He knocked Harry down on the way. Then the shooting began, so we ran outside. The whole house was surrounded by police!

KIM: Was the scar-faced man one of the crooks?

RAY: Yes, he was. So was the man who gave us a ride to the hotel. He was the buying agent from Belko Electronics.

KIM: Belko Electronics? You mean the same company that Charlie Jackson was working for?

RAY: That's right.

TONY: **They were really desperate men. It's a good thing Ray and Mike found me. Otherwise, I'd be at the bottom of the Potomac River right now.**

RAY: **And it's a good thing Kim and Terry called the police. Otherwise, we'd be there with you.**

MIKE: All this excitement has made me very hungry.

TERRY: Well, we've got a cold pizza back at the hotel. You can have it for $8.75.

MIKE: $8.75! For a cold pizza? Well, if that's all there is—

KIM: I've got a better idea. Why don't we all go out for dinner at a fancy restaurant? I think we deserve it!

LISTENING FOR LANGUAGE

Listen to the conversation and fill in the blanks.

See boldface section of previous dialog.

LISTENING AND FUNCTION PRACTICE

Evaluating what has happened. **Sometimes we're happy when someone does something and the results are good. Listen to Tony and Ray's version of what has happened and complete their conversation.**

See boldface section of previous dialog.

READING AND LISTENING FOR SPECIFIC INFORMATION

Now listen to the final conversation with all the friends together at the airport.

RAY: This is the wildest vacation I've ever had. Tony, I guess it was worse for you. What was going through your mind before we got there?

TONY: I was scared stiff.

KIM: Did you expect to come out of it alive?

TONY: Well, I wasn't exactly optimistic, but I hoped I could work out a deal with Wilbur. I could tell he wasn't happy with the way things were going.

TERRY: In a way, Wilbur saved the day, didn't he?

TONY: Yeah, it all happened so fast. When he knocked Harry over, the gun fell to the floor, so I jumped up and headed for the door as fast as I could.

TERRY: You're lucky that the gun didn't go off accidentally.

MIKE: Were you surprised when we showed up in the basement?

TONY: I'll say. I didn't think you were even worried about me. I thought you were all out having a good time. You know, I'm glad about Wilbur. He may not even have to go to jail.

RAY: Yeah, well I'm really glad Kim persuaded me to come along on this trip. How come I never saw any of you on campus before?

TERRY: Middletown isn't exactly a small school, you know.

TONY: Yeah. You know, Dr. Franklin felt so bad about this whole thing that she offered me a company scholarship. They're going to pay my way through the rest of school and I'm going to work for them full-time when I graduate. I won't have to work twenty hours a week anymore.

KIM: More time for fun.

RAY: You know, we should plan to get together after school starts.

MIKE: Yeah. We can sit around and talk about what a great time we all had—especially Tony.

TONY: Right! Well, I wouldn't say I had a *great* time, but, for sure, this is one vacation I'll never forget!

Answer Key

Lesson 1
LISTENING WITH A PURPOSE

1. to get aspirin
2. It's small and green.
3. It looks like Tony's.

LISTENING FOR IMPORTANT DETAILS

1. True   2. True   3. True   4. True
5. False   6. True

LISTENING FOR LANGUAGE

1. didn't   2. did   3. got   4. get   5. was
6. comes   7. get   8. does   9. It's
10. mine

LISTENING AND FUNCTION PRACTICE

Part 1.

KIM: Terry, _I'd like you to meet Tony_.
Tony, _this is my friend Terry_ .
TONY: _It's nice to meet you_ .
TERRY: _Nice to meet you too_ .
Where are you from?
TONY: Right here in Miami. _How about you_ ?
TERRY: I'm from Miami too.

Part 2.

A: (*Student B's name*), I'd like you to meet (*Student C*). (*Student C*), this is (*Student B*).

B: _It's nice to meet you_ .
C: _It's nice to meet you too_ .
B: Where are you from?
C: (*Student C's country*). How about you?
B: I'm from (*Student B's country*).

READING AND LISTENING FOR SPECIFIC INFORMATION

1. a   2. b   3. a   4. b

Terry said Tony went to get some aspirin. Mike said he went to get something to eat. Terry is right.

Lesson 2
PREDICTING 4

LISTENING FOR IMPORTANT DETAILS

1. False   2. False   3. False   4. True
5. True

LISTENING FOR LANGUAGE

1. to   2. us   3. don't   4. he   5. a   6. Did
7. he   8. without

LISTENING FOR MAIN IDEAS

b, e

LISTENING AND FUNCTION PRACTICE

1. b   2. a   3. b   4. b   5. a   6. b   7. a

READING AND LISTENING FOR DIFFERENT POINTS OF VIEW

1. isn't   2. is   3. Terry

Lesson 3
PREDICTING 2

LISTENING FOR IMPORTANT DETAILS

1. a   2. c   3. b   4. a   5. a

LISTENING FOR LANGUAGE

1. about   2. he   3. we   4. the   5. felt
6. had   7. can   8. a   9. know   10. does
11. Who   12. found

INTENSIVE LISTENING

Mike: two cheeseburgers, french fries, onion rings, a chocolate shake
Ray: an egg salad sandwich, black coffee
Kim: fried chicken dinner, mashed potatoes and gravy, cheesecake, diet cola

LISTENING AND FUNCTION PRACTICE

1. b 2. a 3. a 4. b 5. a 6. b 7. a

READING AND LISTENING FOR DIFFERENT POINTS OF VIEW

He thought it was strange that Terry's suitcase was in the trash can.
1. He thinks Terry has done something wrong.
2. no

Lesson 4
LISTENING WITH A PURPOSE

1. a stranger who looked like the man who brought them to the hotel
2. microfilm

LISTENING FOR IMPORTANT DETAILS

1. True 2. True 3. True 4. False
5. False 6. True 7. False

LISTENING FOR SEQUENCE OF EVENTS

6, 1, 2, 8, 4, 5, 3, 9, 7

LISTENING FOR LANGUAGE

1. There's 2. who 3. What 4. Come
5. on 6. can 7. are 8. help

LISTENING AND FUNCTION PRACTICE

MIKE: Did you hurt yourself?
TERRY: Oh, my foot.
MIKE: Let me help you up.
TERRY: I'm OK now.

READING AND LISTENING FOR SPECIFIC INFORMATION

the man who gave them a ride to the hotel
1. Wilbur's boss. 2. They are probably criminals. 3. no

Lesson 5
LISTENING FOR IMPORTANT DETAILS

1. False 2. False 3. True 4. True
5. False 6. False 7. True

LISTENING FOR LANGUAGE

1. it 2. It 3. it 4. this 5. this 6. it
7. Those

LISTENING FOR MAIN IDEAS

✓ The plans belong to Acme Electronics Corporation.
✓ The battery is inexpensive to produce.
✓ The battery charge lasts for 500 miles if the car is going at 55 miles per hour.

LISTENING AND FUNCTION PRACTICE

1. b 2. a 3. a 4. b 5. b

READING AND LISTENING FOR DIFFERENT POINTS OF VIEW

1. b 2. c 3. b

Lesson 6
PREDICTING

1. the microfilm
2. return the microfilm

LISTENING FOR IMPORTANT DETAILS

1. c 2. d 3. b 4. c 5. d

LISTENING FOR LANGUAGE

1. kind 2. them 3. for 4. no 5. plans
6. his 7. now 8. with 9. staying

INTENSIVE LISTENING

✓ The Washington Monument
✓ The Lincoln Memorial
✓ The Reflecting Pond
✓ The Smithsonian Institution

LISTENING AND FUNCTION PRACTICE

A: Let's **get something to eat**. I'm hungry.
B: That's a good idea, but **we really should go home**.
We can **get something there**.
C: OK.

A: I'm bored. Let's **go**.
B: That's a good idea, but **we really should wait until she serves coffee**.
We can **go home after that**.
C: OK.

READING AND LISTENING FOR SPECIFIC INFORMATION
1. False   2. False   3. True   4. True
5. False

Lesson 7
LISTENING WITH A PURPOSE
1. A member of the gang.
2. She says that the security man won't be there until later that night.

LISTENING FOR IMPORTANT DETAILS
1. False   2. True   3. False   4. True
5. False   6. False

LISTENING FOR LANGUAGE
1. have   2. don't   3. hungry   4. not
5. phone   6. delivers   7. medium
8. extra

LISTENING FOR SEQUENCE OF EVENTS
2 Mike orders a pizza.
4 A man takes the microfilm from the students.
1 The students return to the hotel.
5 Dr. Franklin calls.
3 Terry complains about her headache.
6 Mike and Ray run after the man who took the microfilm.

LISTENING AND FUNCTION PRACTICE
Part 1.
S Why don't we order a pizza?
S The way you eat, I think we should get an extra large.
Part 2.
1. b   2. a   3. a   4. b   5. a

READING AND LISTENING FOR SPECIFIC INFORMATION
1. Harry   2. Harry
3. Charlie Jackson tapped Dr. Franklin's phone.
4. She thought they lost the scar-faced man.

Lesson 8
PREDICTING
1. They follow the man to a house and think they see Tony inside.   2. no
LISTENING FOR IMPORTANT DETAILS
1. False   2. False   3. False   4. False
5. True   6. False

LISTENING FOR LANGUAGE
1. helping   2. watching   3. aren't
4. parked   5. after   6. went   7. one
8. it   9. Let's

LISTENING FOR DETAILS C
✓ has big ears
✓ has a short tail
✓ has big teeth
✓ has strange spots

LISTENING AND FUNCTION PRACTICE
1. looks like   2. tastes like
3. sounds like   4. seems like
5. feels like   6. smells like

READING AND LISTENING FOR DIFFERENT POINTS OF VIEW
Mike's like a brother to her.
She likes Ray.
1. True   2. False
Terry thinks they were always just good friends. Mike thinks that they were boyfriend and girlfriend at first.

Lesson 9
PREDICTING
1. the security man   2. the pizza man

LISTENING FOR IMPORTANT DETAILS
1. True   2. True   3. False   4. True
5. False

LISTENING FOR LANGUAGE
1. from   2. see   3. up   4. don't
5. mean   6. is   7. gave   8. ago   9. him
10. look   11. and

LISTENING AND MAKING INFERENCES
1. RAY: Hi Kim, this is Ray.
2. RAY: We're at a phone booth near 367 Mulberry Street. We saw the man go into a house.
3. RAY: We saw someone tied up. It might be Tony.
4. RAY: In the basement.
5. RAY: OK, we're at 367 Mulberry Street.
6. RAY: We're going to go in after him now.

LISTENING AND FUNCTION PRACTICE
1. a   2. b   3. b

READING AND LISTENING FOR SPECIFIC INFORMATION

1. a 2. b 3. a
1. His plane was late.
2. The taxi driver drove very slowly and went around in circles.

Lesson 10
LISTENING WITH A PURPOSE

1. in the basement of the house
2. The crooks didn't want him to escape.
3. kill him

LISTENING FOR IMPORTANT DETAILS

1. c 2. b 3. c 4. a 5. c 6. a

LISTENING FOR LANGUAGE

1. feeling 2. accident 3. going
4. trying 5. get 6. said 7. up 8. let's

LISTENING FOR ROLES AND RELATIONSHIPS

J He is guarding Tony.
H He took the microfilm from Tony's friends.
H Tony's friends thought he was the security man from Acme.
C He put the microfilm in Tony's suitcase.
W He is the buying agent for Belko Electronics.
W He parked the car in the parking garage.
C He drove Tony to the airport.
W He doesn't want to kill anybody.

LISTENING AND FUNCTION PRACTICE

1. as 2. as 3. good 4. as 5. as
6. nice 7. delicious/good 8. much
9. many

READING AND LISTENING FOR DIFFERENT POINTS OF VIEW

Tony thinks his friends are not worried about him and are out having a good time. Terry says they are all worried sick about him.

Lesson 11
PREDICTING

✓ Mike and Ray will find Tony.
✓ Tony will be rescued by Mike and Ray.
✓ The police will come.

LISTENING FOR IMPORTANT DETAILS

1. False 2. True 3. False 4. True
5. False

LISTENING FOR LANGUAGE

1. can 2. back 3. that 4. down
5. that 6. Am 7. out 8. These 9. way

LISTENING FOR SEQUENCE OF EVENTS

First, the crooks will make Tony **write a suicide note**.
Next, the crooks will **make a copy of the film** and put it **in Tony's pocket**.
Then they will throw Tony, Mike and Ray **into the river**.
The police will find **Tony** with **the film** and Mike and Ray **there too**.
Finally, the police will **close the case**.

LISTENING AND FUNCTION PRACTICE

1. b 2. a 3. b 4. b

READING AND LISTENING FOR SPECIFIC INFORMATION

1. False 2. True 3. True
✓ Tony had a headache on the plane.
✓ Tony disappeared at the airport.
✓ The police know where Tony is.

Lesson 12
PREDICTING

1. They will escape. 2. no 3. no

LISTENING FOR IMPORTANT DETAILS

1. True 2. False 3. True 4. True
5. False

LISTENING FOR LANGUAGE

1. what 2. When 3. me 4. next
5. were 6. How 7. there 8. working
9. our 10. them 11. When 12. would

LISTENING FOR MAIN IDEAS

☑ He was working for Belko Electronics.
☑ He took Tony to the airport.
☑ He was friendly to Tony.
☑ He had a more important job than Tony at Acme.
☑ He knew Harry.
☑ He talked to Tony about his trip to Washington.

LISTENING AND FUNCTION PRACTICE

Part 1.
1. It's a good thing 2. Otherwise 3. It's a good thing 4. Otherwise

Part 2.
1. It's a good thing you offered me a ride. Otherwise, I'd
2. It's a good thing you came back for your umbrella. Otherwise, I'd

READING AND LISTENING FOR SPECIFIC INFORMATION

1. False 2. False 3. False 4. True

After the lights went out, Wilbur got scared and tried to run out .

He bumped into Harry and knocked him over and the gun fell to the floor .

Tony jumped up and ran to the door.

Acknowledgements

We would like to express our sincerest gratitude to the following people for their help in many different ways in successfully completing this project:

Brian Anderson, Annette Fawbush, Patrick Kameen, Kathryn Lance, Daphna Levit-Lance, Jay Mauer, Raymond J. Raymond and Joseph Sheehan